THE NEVER-ENDING STREAM

A Tribute to Fly-Tying Form and Function

Scott Sanchez

PRUETT PUBLISHING COMPANY
BOULDER, COLORADO

www.pruettpublishing.com

First Edition 2010

ISBN 0-87108-945-9

Library of Congress Cataloging-in-Publication Data available on request

All photographs and illustrations by Scott Sanchez

Design by Kay Turnbaugh

Printed in Korea

Contents

INTRODUCTION

Fly-tying ideas are like an ever-changing stream, constantly flowing and picking up momentum from various sources.

At the headwaters of a trout stream, ribbons of snowmelt
converge to form the initial brook.

The snowmelt flows down, gaining volume from tributaries and evolving in size and diversity, until it becomes a sizeable river.

Tributaries are its source of energy. Some are constant, while others are seasonal.

Some significantly increase the river's volume, while others add an important trickle of cool water to a warm summer river.

Springs, created by the stream's percolation, come back to augment
the stream's flow and moderate its temperatures.

The importance of tributaries will vary with year and season, and
all tributaries will contribute at differing levels.

Back eddies recycle the flow and bring water back upstream
to surge downstream again.

Side channels meander in different directions from the main flow but converge again to enhance it. Sometimes it is hard to determine which current is a side channel and which is the stream.

At different times along its course, the water is a raging torrent, and at others times it is a slow pool; however, it still maintains its own character and is unique among other waters.

Eventually, this stream will supply its resources to another, and ultimately it will become part of an ocean.

So it is with fly tying—the convergence of tributary concepts and fishing experiences forms our basic stream of ideas, and through the contributions of others, we add to our river of knowledge, technique, and ideas. These influences can be direct or indirect—a personal friend, time spent with another, or through reading a magazine article or book. Some influences contribute constantly to our river of ideas, while others give us a quick, important surge. Sometimes we drift off on tangents, but we bring back those concepts to add to our main stream. Some ideas hide in the back of our mind until they are needed. Unbiased comments from others give us a perspective and help us fine-tune our flies. Those we teach in turn become our teachers. Patterns change; they adapt and pick up flow and energy until they become our latest realization. However, unlike the trout stream, fly-tying ideas never end—they keep moving and evolving.

While I have a reputation as an innovative flytier, my patterns wouldn't exist without the ideas and help of others. We all build upon the past and present to achieve our current set of ideas.

I'm always amazed at the artistic abilities of skilled flytiers. When you look at traditional art and a well-tied fly, there is a correlation: good fly tying is art. This isn't art in the esoteric fashion, although some facets like traditional Atlantic salmon fly tying would fall into that category. This is utilitarian sculpture much like the work achieved by an expert cabinetmaker, knife maker, or gunsmith. They are beautiful but are meant to be used. They give pleasure from appearance and function. Design is part of the art as well as the execution. Like many functional art forms, a good chunk of the artistry involved in fishing flies comes from the simplicity and effectiveness. Less can be more, especially when it is done to perfection.

In this book, I would like to give tribute to the individuals and flies that are the significant tributaries to my fly tying.

THE ALLENS

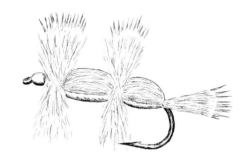

Allen Double Humpy

FOR THE BETTER PART OF A CENTURY, three generations of the Allens have been at the leading edge of flies and guiding on Jackson Hole's Snake River. These three generations have been involved with the evolution of the popular western pattern, the Humpy, a living legacy of the rough-and-tumble rivers of the Rocky Mountains. The exact beginnings of the Humpy are somewhat vague, and there is a good possibility that it may have been coinvented in various places of the West for similar waters. Dan Bailey's Goofus Bug and Jack Horner's Horner Deer Hair are certainly parallel patterns, but Boots Allen seems to be the father of the Jackson-style Humpy.

I knew of the Humpy and had seen it in the sporting goods stores of Salt Lake City. However, it was on a Boy Scout trip to Jackson, Wyoming, in 1973 that I saw my first original. As the standard tourists, we had to make a tour of the town square with its elk antler arches. Located on the square was the old Jackson Sporting Goods, and a trip inside brought me to the fly counter and a jar of official Boots Allen Humpies. I bought one for a sample, and when I made it home, I started tying them. Later on I learned the refined method of tying from Jack Dennis's books.

I first met Boots in 1984 just after I had moved to Jackson and was working at Jackson Ski and Sports. Every week, Boots would come by with a supply of worms and sucker meat for the bait fishermen in the area. He also would stock the glass jars with his flies. These included some buggy-looking Humpies and Mormon Girl Streamers. Many times they weren't even tied on fly hooks; instead, they were fashioned on whatever hooks Boots had lying around. In spite of their less-than-perfect appearance, Boots's flies were legendary, and customers would come in looking for them. In discussions with Boots, he would tell you why you needed to buy, sell, and fish local flies instead of the imported varieties. Much of my early knowledge of fishing the Snake River and area lakes came from conversations with Boots. Boots always had a story. One of the best was making money by selling leeches to doctors. To accomplish this, he would wade into a pond near Jackson Lake with bare legs. He would stay in there until he had enough leeches on his body, then he would get out, put the leeches in jars, and take them to town.

Leonard Raymond "Boots" Allen was born in 1910 near the Kentucky–Indiana border. Boots moved to Jackson in 1927 to work on Jackson Lake Dam and built up the riprap for three years. One of his jobs was to float and clear dam debris. This was the start of his career on the Snake River. As Boots would say in later times, "I spent three years building it and the rest of my life wanting to see it come down."

In the winter of 1928–1929, Boots started doing snow-survey work for the Bureau of Reclamation. I can remember him telling stories of using wooden skis with elk-hair climbing skins to access the sites, and wintering in remote cabins near Jackson Lake. To supplement his food supplies, he would ice fish for lake trout. Boots consumed some of these, but he also traded fish to ranchers for beef. He married his wife Gail in 1937, and soon after, their daughter Saundra was born. With a baby, they wanted to be closer to medical care and schools, so at this point, they moved into Jackson. Boots had been a guide since 1932 to supplement his income, and after moving to Jackson in 1937, he began to guide for a full-time seasonal job. In the evenings, he worked as a blackjack dealer at the Wort Hotel, which also put him in contact with potential clients. At the time, Bob Carmichael was the only established outfitter. Beyond that, there were only a couple of guides in the area.

In 1945, Boots moved into the official outfitting and tackle business to complement his guiding. He called his enterprise Fort Jackson and located it near the town square. With the short Jackson sum-

Yellow Humpy, Double Humpy, Rubber Leg Double Humpy

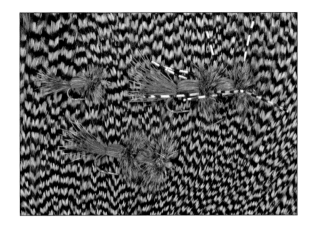

mer season, you had to be versatile; therefore, besides being in the fishing business, Fort Jackson did scenic floats, rented trailer parking spots, and sold fireworks. Boots was now supporting three children, who included the future guides Dick and Joe. Boots was well known for his Humpies, but as early as the 1940s, he was tying a stonefly nymph called the Gros Ventre Nymph. He didn't originate the Mormon Girl Streamer, but his version was one of the most popular Jackson streamers for decades. Boots was concerned with getting kids out fishing and was involved in many activities that put kids on the water. Many top Jackson guides had their early starts with Fort Jackson, usually first as shop help and then as guides. Even Jack Dennis had an early start in the fishing business working for Boots.

For years, Boots had a bait and fly shop in his garage. All transactions were on the honor system, and you would drop the money in the jar for whatever you bought. One time, someone robbed the money jar. If anyone had caught the thief, there would have been a lynch mob in town. When Boots passed away in 1993, many of the townspeople of Jackson showed up to pay their respects. The church was full. Boots was one of the last of the fishing pioneers in the valley.

At a young age, Dick and Joe became involved in the business and eventually took over most of the operation. With their father's experience and time on the water, they became sought-out guides. Joe was also a prolific flytier. His mistake—the Double Humpy—became a regional favorite.

The Double Humpy is the second-generation Jackson Humpy and came out of Joe's vise by mistake. The Allens tied the flies sold at Fort Jackson and spent a good part of the winter tying their creations. They also sold them to other local shops. Anyone who has spent time filling orders understands that sometimes your hands go on autopilot as your mind drifts off. And that is how the Double Humpy came about. During the winter of 1980–1981, after tying gobs of Humpies, Joe switched to tying hoppers on a longer shank hook. Except his fingers tied another Humpy on the rear of the hook. Instead of tossing the fly, he added another Humpy on the front end.

Thus the Double was born. Some blame it on "head cement," while others call it fate. For years, the Double Humpy owned the large attractor-fly market in Jackson, and it is still a great fly today. You could always pick out Joe's Double Humpy. It was bushy, heavily hackled, and a little rough around the edges. Who knows what it imitated—maybe mating bugs, a bug cluster, a fluttering stonefly, or a rib-eye steak—but fish liked to eat it. This was the only fly that many anglers fished. Most fished it as a dry fly, but it can be effective when it is stripped under the surface or dead drifted and then stripped at the end of the drift.

I remember a time during my early years at the Jack Dennis Shop when we ran out of Double Humpies in the middle of the summer. Jack tied some to fill the bins. They were beautiful and were immaculately tied. The next day, the guides came in and, under their breath, said, "We need some Joe Allen Double Humpies—Jack's nice ones don't work." This made me think about intentionally having some rough ends on large attractors. It seems to work.

Joe was a character and was always good for an off-color story or joke, but if you listened, you learned a lot about the Snake River and how to fish it. He would introduce himself as "Little Joe from Jackson Hole." Jackson's long winters were rough on Joe, and he spent many of them out of the valley working for his top clients. Joe had a following.

Dick and Joe Allen were definitely not fly-fishing purists, and many of their trips focused on spin or even bait fishing. Sometimes they got a bad rap from newcomers about catch and release. Joe could be a wiseass, but his bark was much worse than his bite. The reality is, they cared for the resource as much as anyone. Fort Jackson and Boots financed most of the work at the Wilson Bridge boat launch, and Boots was instrumental in approaching the county and Wyoming Game and Fish Department about improvements that benefited a myriad of both anglers and recreational floaters.

Allens

(tied by Joseph "Boots" Allen)

YELLOW HUMPY (Boots Allen)

Hook – Standard dry fly, size 6 – 14
Thread – Yellow 3/0
Tail – Natural mule deer hair
Underbody – Tying thread
Body – Natural deer pulled over underbody
Wing – Tips of body hair not separated
Hackle – Heavy grizzly

DOUBLE HUMPY (Joe Allen)

Hook – 3XL streamer, size 4 – 10
Thread – Yellow 3/0
Tail – Natural mule deer hair
Underbodies – Tying thread
Bodies – Natural deer pulled over underbody
Wings – Tips of body hair not separated
Hackles – Heavy grizzly
This is basically two Humpies on one hook.

RUBBER LEG DOUBLE HUMPY (Little Boots Allen)

Hook – 3XL streamer, size 4 – 10
Thread – Yellow 3/0
Tail – Natural mule deer hair
Underbodies – Tying thread
Bodies – Natural deer pulled over underbody
Wings – Tips of body hair not separated
Hackles – Heavy grizzly
This is basically two Humpies on one hook.

Unfortunately, Joe passed away in 2003 at the age of sixty. A back injury from a car accident led to other problems, and long-term health concerns caught up with him. Joe's Double Humpies are now collectors' items.

Enter the Allens, generation three. Although Dick Allen sold Fort Jackson in 1993, members of this generation are still well entrenched in the Jackson fishing scene. As with most family businesses, the kids will spend at least part of their lives involved with their family legacy. Almost all of Dick and Joe's children have guided at one time or another. Joseph Boots Allen, or "Little Boots," took off where his father and grandfather left off and has become one of the preeminent guides in Jackson. As a young guide, he has a stellar reputation, and in both 2003 and 2004, he was the One Fly Guide of the Year, with the highest points of the contest scored by his clients. The Snake River is in his blood. In addition, he is a gifted flytier and has continued the Jackson Humpy tradition with his Rubber-Legged Double Humpy, sold by Orvis, and his Foam Double Humpy, which was picked up by Umpqua Feather Merchants. His Tara X is also a popular guide fly at Will Dornan's Snake River Angler, at which Joseph is a guide. In the last few years, I've spent some time talking with "Little Boots" about flies, fly tying, cameras, and writing. I enjoy exchanging ideas with him. He has published a few articles and is working on a book about Jackson. Of all places to run into another Jacksonite, I've bumped into Boots at the Austin Angler in Austin, Texas. He recently received a Ph.D. from the University of Texas in sociology with a specialization in demography, focusing on rural development and biodiversity. He studied the use of ecotourism as a tool for sustainable development in mountain communities in Kazakhstan and Kyrgyzstan (both part of the former Soviet Union). This of course involved fishing for taimen. His research now focuses on ecological and cultural tourism in Northwest Mongolia. Little Boots's cousin, Tressa, is also an excellent guide and works for the Reel Women guide service. Her brother, Travis, owns the South Fork Skiff Company. ◆

THE BAILEYS

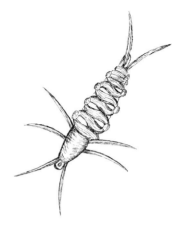

Bailey Mossback

DAN AND JOHN BAILEY HAVE INFLUENCED MY FLIES through their long tradition of fly tying and by my working directly on the Baileys' fly program. For seventy-plus years, the family has been at the forefront of commercial fly production, and many techniques and flies we use today can be traced back to Dan. Likewise, John's expansion of the business brought the tradition of Dan Bailey's flies into the modern age.

I never met Dan in person, but I worked in-house and as a consultant for John Bailey. I became connected with the Bailey operation in the early 1990s. At the time, I was helping Jack Dennis with some flies for Dan Bailey's Fly Shop, and John knew about my tying. We had met a few times, and in September 1993, McKenzie Flies was courting me to be a contract tier. John heard about this and called me from the Denver Fly Tackle Dealer Show. A month later, I drove to Livingston, Montana, met with John, and became a fly consultant for Dan Bailey's. Since that time, I also spent seven years as the wholesale manager, and now that I'm no longer in-house, I'm back in the consulting role.

An automobile mishap may have been one of the greatest blessings to the fly-fishing world. In 1938, the axle on Dan Bailey's car broke on the pass between Livingston and Bozeman, Montana. Dan, with his wife Helen, managed to limp back down the "hill" to Livingston to get their car repaired. While they waited, Dan and Helen decided to stay in Livingston and try to build a future there. The small hole-in-the-wall tackle shop they started that year became the oldest fly shop west of the Mississippi, and for years, the flies tied under its roof made it one of largest fly producers in the world.

Prior to moving to Montana, Dan had been out West a few times and was quick to modify eastern patterns to western conditions and create his own patterns. While living in New York, Dan Bailey became a friend and fishing companion of Lee Wulff. Dan was still living in the East when Lee created the Wulff-style dry. It filled the need for a buoyant pattern to imitate the large eastern mayflies. Lee showed Dan the flies, and Dan convinced Lee to name his flies after himself. When the Baileys came out West, the flotation and visibility of the Wulffs proved invaluable on the large, fast rivers. Originally, Lee had the Grey Wulff and White Wulff. Dan added the Grizzly Wulff and Black Wulff, and Dan's partner, Red Monical, came up with the Blonde Wulff. With Dan and the shop promoting the series, they became standard flies around the world. Dan also added hair tails to the standard dry flies and started the "reversed-hackle" method that is now the standard hackle technique for dries. In this style of hackling, the natural hackle curvature slants forward, which helps balance the tail and hackle of the fly for better support and flotation.

Other important Bailey flies include the Bi-Flies, the Bailey-style Muddler Minnow, the Marabou Muddler, the Bailey Spruce, the braided Nature Flies, the Pop-Eye Streamers, Dan's Deer Hair Hopper, Mylar-bodied streamers, and Bailey's Damsel Fly Nymph. The hairwing Bi-Flies were first created in the East and were made to be both down-wing dries and streamers. You could dead drift them as a stonefly or caddis, and as they swung around, you'd strip them in as a streamer. Many of the modern hairwing stonefly and caddis patterns have roots in the Bi-Fly; the Bi-Fly was also one of the first dry flies to have strike indicators incorporated into it.

Dan Gapen may have originated the Muddler Minnow, but Dan Bailey put it on the map. The Bailey-style Muddler is now the most common version, and Dan's Marabou Muddler spawned multiple generations of mobile sculpin patterns. The Nature Flies were some of the first imitative stonefly nymphs, and the Pop-Eyes were bead heads fifty years before that craze. Bailey was the first whom I know of to use Mylar tubing in freshwater streamers. Dan's Deer Hair Hopper is an improved Joe's Hopper with a body

Dark Olive Mossback

Mossback, John's Elk Hair Hopper

of yellow, flared deer hair, and the hair body extends up through the wings to form an indicator. Here again, Dan was years ahead of the game with indicators on hoppers. The Bailey Spruce was adapted from the Northwest wet fly of the same name. Dan modified it into a streamer, and the addition of grizzly dyed hackle and heavy hackle collar makes it one of the best easy-sinking sculpin patterns. These flies are just the tip of the iceberg of Bailey's fly ideas.

Dan's conservation efforts are as important as his flies, and we can thank him that we have excellent fishing on the waters he started fishing more than seventy years ago. Everyone thinks about the good old days, but the Yellowstone River is cleaner today than it was forty years ago. At one time, mine tailings flowed into the river after rainstorms, sewage was poured into the river at Gardiner and Livingston, and the railroad in Livingston dumped engine-cleaning solvents into the Yellowstone. Dan and other conservationists fought these issues, and we now have a clean and fertile trout fishery on the Yellowstone.

One of Dan's most important conservation projects was the fight against the proposed Allan Spur Dam. This dam would have flooded Paradise Valley and the Spring creeks and restricted the flow on the longest undammed river in the lower forty-eight. He was also involved in the creation of the first Trout Unlimited chapter in Montana and was the national director of Trout Unlimited for a few years. He was also a proponent of public fishing access on Montana's waters. In his memory, the state of Montana issued the Dan and Helen Bailey Conservation Award for deserving recipients.

It is hard to follow in the steps of a famous father, but John Bailey has done well. Dan's business and the business of that era were based on domestic fly production, fly-shop sales, and regional distribution. Many of the fly shops of the time were a combination of a bar, a post office, and a tackle shop. John took over the business at a time when the fly-fishing industry was moving into globalization. In the age of the world economy, you need to adapt—sink or swim. John took the fly business from a small, domestic production to a large-scale import operation. John still ties flies and is critical of quality and design.

There is a good chance that John has fished the fly before it is produced. As both a consultant and in-house sales manager, working on a fly program taught me quite a bit. While fishing and your own commercial tying dictate simplified design, working on a fly program teaches you how to streamline and explain. The greatest fly in the world won't be tied unless you can convey the idea and get consistent materials to the factory. Nothing can be left to interpretation. My material knowledge and sourcing grew. Also, contract tying for Bailey's gave me the world as a fly testing ground. I knew that my flies worked in my waters with my techniques, but I learned about the other places where they worked and got valuable feedback on improvements.

John Bailey has continued his father's legacy of conservation and will take a firm stand even when it is unpopular. He currently heads the Montana Governor's Task Force on the Yellowstone River. John sticks to his guns and says what he thinks. During the flood years of 1996 and 1997, many wanted to dam off a channel of the Yellowstone River that was flowing through Armstrong's and Depuy's Spring creeks. John fought this and believed that if it wasn't right to dam a river for agriculture, it wasn't right to dam it to save recreation.

Through fishing with John, I learned about shooting-head fishing on the Yellowstone to cover water and flies to use for it. While I used heads for lake fishing a variety of sinking lines, I didn't use heads much in moving water. Brown-trout fishing in the fall on the Yellowstone is very similar to steelhead fishing. You wade deep, throw as far as you can, then let the fly swing and strip. This allows you to put a fly in front of a bunch of fish, and it is a very efficient and effective way to cover large pools.

Through John, I also learned the types of flies that are best fished with a shooting head. I certainly like my own rabbit flies, but lighter-weight flies that sink easily are more practical for this kind of fishing. John introduced me to the Bailey- and Chester Marion–style Spruce Flies. He held the heavily hackle-

Bailey

(tied by Dan Bailey's Flies)

DARK OLIVE MOSSBACK   (Dan Bailey)

Hook – 2XL nymph, sizes 4 – 8

Thread – Black A or Nymo

Tail – Two divided dyed dark brown turkey biots

Underbody – Yellow balloon strips

Back – Dyed dark olive and brown monofilament strands

Belly – Dyed light olive and yellow monofilament strands

Thorax – tying thread

Legs – two sets of dyed dark brown turkey biots

JOHN'S ELK HAIR HOPPER   (John Bailey)

Hook – 2XL nymph hook, Size 4 – 12

Thread – Yellow 3/0

Tail – Red deer hair

Body – Yellow poly yarn

Body hackle – brown palmered

Wing – Dark elk

Hackle – Grizzly and brown mixed

collared fly against the current and it came alive. It was wide like a sculpin head, but the fibers pulsated much better than hair or wool. These flies have become an important part of my arsenal for shooting-head fishing.

In the late 1970s, while Dan was still alive, John Bailey hooked up with a fly factory in Bogota, Colombia. The writing was on the wall about domestic fly production. It would always be there, but to satisfy demand, quality flies were needed in volume. Overseas was the answer. However, Bailey's still maintained some production in Livingston for specialty patterns and custom tying. In the late 1990s, a factory in Bhutan was added and eventually became the main source. I went to the Colombia fly factory in 1994 and taught and learned about large-scale fly production. This was in the days when the trip through Miami was more dangerous than the time spent in Bogota. On our return home, the flight was delayed because someone had tried to smuggle a ton of cocaine onto the American flight the day before. Luckily, we were in the legal importing business of flies.

John has tied many different flies, but the patterns for which he is best known are his Elk Hair Hopper and Stonefly. John Bailey created these flies during the high-water period of the late 1970s. He needed a high-floating and more visible stonefly and hopper. Heavy wings of elk hair and thick hackles were put on the flies to address flotation and visibility. The salmon fly was commonly fished with a lightly weighted Bitch Creek Nymph below it. The hopper is still very popular today and also does a good job of imitating golden stones.

Japan also became a source for fly-fishing products. John started importing Dai-Riki leaders in 1983, which were the first of the modern-era, super-strong, copolymer leaders. The name Dai-Riki is owned by Bailey's and translates to "strong." With this connection, Bailey's started importing Dai-Riki hooks in the late 1980s. This was started for fly production, but due to the large number of hooks required to order, it also became a retail item. Dai-Riki hooks have since become a staple with fly shops and commercial tiers.

Dan Bailey's Fly Shop has been in the fly business as long as anyone, and two generations of Baileys have had a major impact on myself and on the rest of the fly-fishing and fly-tying world. ◆

JOHNNY BOYD

Boyd Lightning Dart

JOHNNY BOYD HAS BEEN ONE OF MY BEST FRIENDS for a decade. We met through Dan Bailey's Fly Shop. At the time, I was doing consulting work on their fly program and enjoying the good life in Austin, Texas, by fishing a bunch while my wife went to graduate school. Johnny had just started running the front of the store at Bailey's and, with his extensive tying background, helping on the Bailey fly program. We had talked on the phone many times and were working on flies for production. I first met Johnny briefly at the 1995 Federation of Fly Fishers conclave (FFF) in Livingston, Montana, but it was at the Denver Fly Tackle Dealer Show later that year that we had the chance to spend some time together. As usual, John Bailey booked a suite for the crew to bunk in. I shared the complex with roommates Skip Gibson, the Montana rep, and Johnny Boyd. Both Johnny and I had fly-tying gear and beer in tow, so I knew that this was a good thing. Johnny was working on a fly order, and I was working on ideas for fly production, since we had a couple of the factory people at the show. I watched him tying an order of his Bitch Buggers and Craw Buggers. He effortlessly weaved the chenille bodies and, as opposed to most tiers, each one of them looked perfect. It was obvious from the start that Johnny was at home at the vise.

While Johnny has spent a lifetime as a trout fisherman and tier, he loves fishing for saltwater and warm-water species, and his favorite flies to tie for himself and production are dominated by these fish. I consider him one of the best warm-water/saltwater tiers in the world. His steelhead flies are also pieces of art and reflect his time spent on the water fishing for them. However, I think that pike are his favorite. One of my favorite Montana fishing trips was with Johnny, back to his old haunts in Kalispell, Montana. We spent a few days chasing pike with his buddy, Steve Thompson. We lucked out and had visible pike cruising shallow flats and even ended up with a few doubles. Sometimes when you work together, it is hard to fish together. So this was a real treat. Evenings were spent telling stories at Moose's Saloon. This was old-home day, since Johnny spent a bunch of years in this region.

I've learned quite a few great production-tying tricks from Johnny, and it usually leaves me wondering why I didn't think of that. His knowledge of epoxy and epoxy substitutes is extensive. I picked up using small plastic girl's hair clips to hold the tails on epoxy flies. This keeps the tail from flipping over and landing in the epoxy head of the adjacent fly in the rotisserie. No doubt these were initially borrowed from his daughter, Eliza, who is the same age as my son, Thibaud, and was a frequent playmate of his. The clip method is now standard procedure for me, and it has saved me a bunch of money and time by avoiding rejected flies. Johnny is a master with Body Fur, a synthetic acrylic hackle that can be used to create large bodies. Most tiers create rudimentary flies from the material, but Johnny's are works of art, such as his Diamond Head Snake and Squid. Johnny showed me the intricacies of working with hot glues, which he picked up from Doug Brewer.

His innovative use of plastic lace to create his Lightning Dart series of flies is phenomenal. He has incorporated it in flies ranging from small bait fish to oversized pike patterns. It looks good and is tough, and it catches fish. It is funny that the Lightning Darts were a means of making a heavy version of my Lipstick Minnow. Surprisingly, I found out about them when I visited George Anderson's Yellowstone Angler looking for saltwater fly patterns for my beginners' saltwater tying book. In this book, I wanted to show flies that had representative techniques. I saw the Lightning Dart and said WOW—what a cool fly! I asked Jim Brungardt where they bought these flies, and he said from Johnny. I could surmise the basic tying method, but a trip to Johnny's gave me the gory details. He used a cone for the head and Angel Hair

Boyd's Lightning Dart

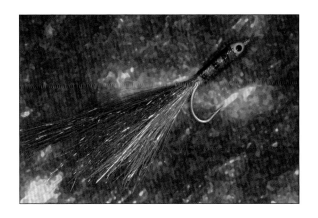

as the underbody and tail. To make the body, he tied in Body Stuff or Jelly Cord and wrapped it over the underbody. The cool part was watching him tie off the body. Instead of using thread to secure it, he wrapped the elastic cord until it broke under the cone. This fused it in place, as the elastic cord wanted to expand under the cone. Just another of the man's simple but great ideas.

This fly saved my butt once on a 2002 trip to the Florida Keys. As usual, a cold front followed me and it was colder in Islamorada than it was in Livingston, Montana. Of course, this made fishing a little tough. Robert "Bobby the

Boyd

LIGHTNING DART ALL PURPOSE CHUB MINNOW (tied by Johnny Boyd)

Hook – Dai-Riki 930 or 810 standard saltwater, size 1/0 – 2
Thread – Tan Flat Waxed Nylon
Head – silver ¼-inch conehead
Lower Tail – Silver Angel Hair
Mid tail – Light Brown Angel Hair
Top tail – Turquoise Angel Hair
Underbody – Tying thread built up over tail material to form smooth underbody
Overbody – Silver fleck Large Body Stuff colored with turquoise marker and
coated with epoxy
Eyes – Painted yellow with black pupils on cone

Butcher" DeAngeles and I got a tip about tarpon fishing the lights around the bridges on a north-wind-accentuated, outgoing tide. This washes bait fish and shrimp off the flats in quantity. The highlight of the night adventure was swinging a Lightning Dart and having a tarpon suck it in. She jumped a few times, and eventually, I had her against the riprap. I went down and grabbed the shock tippet just as she made a final flop and the hook pulled—short-distance release. That was the closest we made it to a saltwater fish on that trip. Thanks, Johnny.

With his Bitch Buggers and Craw Buggers, Johnny uses Montana-style braided bodies and marabou to fool large trout and bass. They are very popular with regional guides. His cone-headed rabbit streamers also have a following. Although big predator flies are his favorite, he can tie a spring-creek fly with equal ease. He is a well-versed tier. Another of Johnny's great ideas is his removable monofilament weed guard. He attaches hollow vinyl tubing, such as Larvae Lace, to the bend of the hook and to just behind the hook's eye. A strand of mono can be inserted into the tubing to make a mono-loop weed guard. This allows you to fish the same fly in different situations and is great on warmwater and flats flies. Besides being an innovative tier, Johnny also produces a number of flies for his clients. His tying room/combination den of death is a classic, with organized bins of materials, fishing, hunting gear, and mountain-man gear. Whenever I go over to his place, his wife Michelle tells me that he is down in the tying room. The man is a fly-tying machine.

Johnny was born and raised in Libby, Montana, near the well-known trophy fishery of the Kootenai River, and spent his youth fishing and hunting. He has some great stories of chasing oversized bull trout in small creeks near his home, in the days before this was restricted. I asked when he started tying and he commented, "I tell everyone I was eight years old. That's pretty close. I know Nixon was president and Little League baseball was very important to me." Soon afterwards, the Libby locals started bringing him materials to tie and modify their favorite flies. He said, "I initially didn't have enough brains to charge anything." Shortly after this he got wise, and a lifetime career was started.

Like most of us, Johnny worked various odd jobs in his youth, including delivering pizza, setting pins briefly in a bowling alley, and working on a salvage crew for train derailments (lumber, wheat, TVs, etc.). He did these jobs until he realized that retail sporting goods sales was a better way to support his fishing, hunting, and fly-tying habits. At nineteen, he had an in-home fly shop called Boyd's Backroom and one called Vimy Ridge Sports. The sporting goods industry is another of his constant careers, and he continues to work in it today. Over the years he has been a store manager, a buyer, and a sales rep. If you ever want someone to negotiate a deal, he is the one because he has seen business from all the angles and is very good at it.

A hobby out of hand caused him to create his Montana Tie'm tying company in 1997. This condensed his manufacturing, sales, and consulting into one company. When Frontier Flies was in business, he became a contract tier for them, and since this was during his sales rep days, he was able to sell his flies as well. This is a smart man who can double dip in that business. Over the years, he has consulted for Bernie Griffin of Griffin Tools. He even taught Bernie's daughter to tie flies. His vast knowledge of tying and retail has helped put Griffin tying tools at the top.

I'm sure that on my next trip to Johnny's tying room I'll learn a new trick. ◆

Charlie Brooks

Brooks Montana Stone

I NEVER MET CHARLIE BROOKS IN PERSON, but his writings on nymph fishing the greater Yellowstone area are thoroughly integrated into my tying and fishing. I learned about Charlie Brooks from a friend of mine, Bernie "Dubs" Horgan. Dubs is one of the best nymph fishermen, and a pathological angler, hunter, and cowboy—with a pharmaceutical degree to support his habits. Charlie Brooks's writings and flies took my nymph fishing and tying from a simple form to an extensive array of methods, and my beat-up copies of *Trout and the Stream* and *Nymph Fishing for Larger Trout* are underlined like a college textbook. His methods were the first I had seen on nymphing the heavy currents found in my area's streams, and his imitations also covered the insects found in those waters. This wasn't Pennsylvania nymphing—it was fishing the waters in my backyard and imitating the bugs in my neighborhood. His in-the-round concept and heavy weighting are the basis of many of my flies. *Fishing Yellowstone Waters* fast-forwarded my learning curve and tempted me to try many of the Yellowstone National Park's waters. Without that book, it would have taken years of research. Nymph fishing was a fairly well-covered subject, but Charlie put a special Greater Yellowstone twist on it.

I first read *Nymph Fishing for Larger Trout* on a trip from Jackson to San Jose in April 1986 to see a friend of mine, Tim Williams, who was on spring break from San Jose State University. The plan was to goof off and see what kind of California fish we could catch. On the way to the airport, I stopped by Jack Dennis Sports to pick up an airplane read and bought a copy of *Nymph Fishing for Larger Trout*. I remembered that Dubs Horgan had recommended it the last time we fished. It ended up being much more than an occupier of time. I read it and reread it on the flights. I was captivated by the knowledge in the pages and how it related to the waters in my area. The book was earmarked, highlighted, and in rough shape by the time I landed in California. When Tim picked me up at the airport, he had heard rumors of salmon flies on the Merced River near Yosemite. That sounded good to me, especially since these bugs were two months away back home. By dumb luck, after reading Brooks's book, I was fishing the river where he first saw an artificial nymph fished—the Merced. I tried his different methods and caught some fish, although I didn't knock them dead. I needed more practice. When I made it home, I had more time to try the methods and tie the flies. And, of course, I bought a collection of his books.

Charlie Brooks started tying and fly fishing in 1930 at the age of nine in the Missouri Ozarks. From here, he would travel on to become one of the best-known writers and anglers in the Greater Yellowstone Region. At the time, overall nymph fishing was a crude art in the West and even across the country. Charlie was responsible for bringing western nymph fishing to a whole generation of anglers.

Charlie's first career was in the U.S. Air Force. He also spent a short time between his Air Force gigs as a ranger in Yosemite National Park, which fueled his interest in fly fishing. Through a traveling angler, he saw his first nymph, a cased caddis imitation. After this, he reentered the U.S. Air Force so that he would be able to retire at a young age and fish the rest of his life. Most other jobs would have delayed his fishing profession. Trips to Yellowstone National Park helped him decide he needed to live in the area after retirement, and in 1964, after retiring, he built a home near West Yellowstone, Montana. This was the start of his second career of fishing, studying water and insects, and then ultimately writing about them. He wrote magazine articles and was a speaker at banquets. His books, *Larger Trout for the Western Fly Fisherman*, *The Trout and the Stream*, *Nymph Fishing for Larger Trout*, *Fishing Yellowstone Waters*, and *The Henry's Fork*, are well-written classics, and although they were written in the 1970s and 1980s, they still have merit today.

Brooks Montana Stone

Charlie's interest in nymph fishing led him into researching the insects that lived in his local waters. Through diligent reading and contact with amateur and professional entomologists, he learned the tricks of the trade. He seined various waters and thoroughly documented his findings. To see how the insects appeared and to observe their behavior, he donned a face mask and made a breathing tube out of a hose. This allowed him to see what the trout did as well. Through his underwater studies, he came up with his "in-

Brooks

MONTANA STONE (tied by Scott Sanchez)

Hook – 4XL heavy streamer, sizes 4 – 8
Thread – Black Nymo 3/0
Tail – Crow or raven primary fibers
Body – Black four–strand fuzzy yarn
Hackle – One grizzly and one grizzly dyed brown
Gills – Light grey or white ostrich herl

the-round" theory for fast-water artificial nymphs. He noticed that actual nymphs didn't tumble in the current but instead reacted by trying to get back down in the substrata. From a trout's view, the dark back of the insect was visible, not the lighter belly. In contrast, a dead-drifted, inanimate artificial would tumble in the current. To always present the trout with the familiar dark back, he started tying his flies "in the round." This caused the fly to look natural and show its correct side no matter how much it rolled. This method started with his large stonefly imitations but also made it into his subsurface mayflies. The Brooks Stone, or, as Charlie called it, the Montana Stone, and his Yellow Stone are the best known of these flies and in later years were produced by commercial tying operations. Of course, most caddis larvae, cased or uncased, have a symmetrical appearance and color, so the "in the round" works for them as well.

Another beauty of the Brooks patterns is their simplicity. When you fished sinking lines and weighted nymphs most of the time, you were going to make some donations to the fish gods. His flies were quick to tie, which is representative of an angling tier.

Brooks's in-the-round flies have had a serious impact on my tying and fishing. My home water the Snake River, the South Fork in Idaho, and the Henry's Fork have a preponderance of large stoneflies. After seeing Brown Stone shucks all over on the Snake, I worked on creating some big stonefly nymphs. I tied up some Brooks Stone and then used it as a template for my Chez Sparkle Stone, and because of reading *Nymph Fishing for Larger Trout*, I learned how, when, and where to fish the big stone nymph patterns. My Ultra Zug nymph series, which have traveled the world and fooled numbers of fish for myself and others, have a basis in Charlie Brooks's in-the-round idea. His Skunk Hair Caddis was the first cased caddis larvae that I saw, which was dark enough to imitate the dominate *Brachycentrus* and related species of caddis found in the Greater Yellowstone Region. It took awhile to evolve, but my Glass House Caddis can trace its lineage to that pattern.

Brooks is best known for his big nymphs, but he had many other innovative patterns that were ahead of their time. His Natan Nylon Nymph is one of the first foam-floating nymph patterns. Due to material constraints of the era he had to encase Styrofoam in a panty-hose bubble. He also had crickets and hoppers with Styrofoam bodies more than thirty years ago. What would have happened if the foams were common today? His original Cream Wiggler used an extended rubber-leg body, and it was one of the first extended rubber-body flies. Brooks's Quill Body Minnow made me think about using poppers on trout. This certainly isn't conventional, but it is pretty entertaining watching trout blow up on the surface and occasionally having Jaws show up.

As the years go by, I experiment with new and different flies, but Charlie Brooks's ideas still form a solid foundation in my patterns. ◆

Jay Buchner

Buchner Dun Caddis

Jay Buchner is one of the most talented tiers in the Rockies. He ties immaculate flies of many varieties, but he also brings to the table an extensive knowledge of regional aquatic insect life. This combination scares the trout but benefits the angler. It is easier to imitate an insect when you know what you are looking at. Basically, why take an out-of-focus photo? Through Jay, I've learned a lot about the bug life of Jackson, Wyoming, and this has helped me to create flies that imitate the important characteristics of the naturals and, by doing so, fool fish. Jay's knowledge of regional aquatic insects is an important part of my fly patterns and fishing.

I met Jay in the fall of 1984 just after I had moved to Jackson. I was a young kid learning the area, and was on the drive back from one of my first trips to Flat Creek. At the time, Jay owned High Country Flies, and the small shop was on the north end of town. I pulled in. It was a fly shop that I hadn't visited, so I had to take a look. Besides the standard array of tackle, there was a great selection of shop-packaged tying materials and some very nice flies. This was a brief visit with a short chat, but later I would get to know Jay much better.

As I spent more time in Jackson, different people commented on the tying and fishing skills of Jay and his wife, Kathy. About that time, I saw a copy of the *Second Fly Tyers Almanac.* A section of the book was on the Buchners and their flies. I ran into Jay at the local Trout Unlimited events and at the One Fly and started to get to know him. He found out that I was a flytier and we had quite a few good chats. In the early 1990s, I served with him on the Jackson Trout Unlimited board and therefore spent quite a bit of time in his company. As the newest board member, the task of organizing the annual banquet fell on my shoulders. Those who have served on nonprofits know the ploy. Fortunately, Jay was helpful, and the banquet went off very well. At this time, we talked flies and fishing quite a bit, and I found out that he was also the aquatic bug guru in Jackson. One project that we worked on together was the first Kids' Fishing Day at the Jackson Visitors' Center pond. Jay seined some bugs out of the pond, and I think I was one of the most interested kids.

I gleaned a vast amount of local entomology information from Jay, and he was more than willing to teach. He explained the behavior of the large brown stones of which I found shucks on the Snake River. He told me that the *Claassenia* stones had a nocturnal emergence and that the males had only part of a wing; this is why they would run across the water when caught. It was also one of the reasons why actively fished big dries worked so well and why a big rubber leg like a Brown Yuk Bug was a good pattern to fish along the banks in the morning. I also learned that the large tan mayflies that hatched in August and September were *Hecuba* and were cousins to the Green Drake. My original Chez Sparkle Stone and Spandex Stone have a foundation in my absorbed knowledge of the *Claassenia,* and the information of the *Hecuba* pushed my learning adaptation of Wulff and parachute patterns.

Since that time, we have had many good discussions on entomology and fly design. I can distinctly remember one discussion we had at the Shilo Inn Bar in Idaho Falls. While we were looking at freshly hatched spring *Baetis* on the windows, we talked about the fact that most mayfly dun imitations were probably better cripples. It is hard to perfectly imitate the precise footprint of a dun, but the tails, bodies, and hackles of the artificials emulate the shape of cripples. Maybe we had boxes and boxes of cripples, but we concluded that the trout *liked* to eat the cripples.

Jay's Dry Stone Fly, Dun Caddis

Jay grew up in eastern Iowa and spent much of his youth fishing. Family trips to Michigan and Ontario, Canada, gave him a chance to expand his fishing experience and skills. When he was eight, he learned how to tie flies from his grandfather. Another one of his interests was falconry, and this hobby eventually brought him out to Wyoming. Jay worked as a bird-of-prey handler for Mutual of Omaha's *Wild Kingdom* TV show. When he decided to go to college, falconry was a catalyst in the decision. He found out that there was a

Buchner

(tied by Jay Buchner)

JAY'S DRY STONE FLY

Hook – Mustad 90240 light wire up eye
　　　　salmonfly hook, size 4 – 8
Thread – Yellow 3/0
Tail – Elk mane
Body – Light yellow polypropylene yarn
Body hackle – Badger trimmed to half a gap
Wing – Elk mane
Head and collar – Natural deer

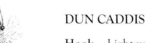

DUN CADDIS

Hook – Light wire dry fly, sizes 8 – 20
Thread – Grey 8/0
Body – Natural grey goose secondary wing fibers
Wing – Two dun hen feathers
Antennae – Stems of wing feather
Hackle – Oversized dun hackle trimmed on top and bottom

big group of falconers at the University of Wyoming (UW), and the birding was much better than in Iowa. It was off to Laramie. While he was attending UW he even met Jacques Herter, the son of the Herter's catalog tycoon, George Leonard Herter.

During his college years, he worked for a Jackson family, whom he met in Laramie. His summer work was putting up buck-rail fence in Bondurant, Wyoming. Although this was hard work, it gave him the chance to spend time outdoors and see the area. After college in the late 1960s, he moved to Jackson.

Jay met his wife, Kathy, in Jackson. She did the typical Jackson thing—she went there for a summer job and never left. She had fished with her father many times in Utah's Uinta Mountains, and after she met Jay, she learned to tie flies.

Jay worked as a guide, tied flies, and gave tying lessons, which eventually led him to start High Country Flies in 1974. Jay continued to guide, and for a while, even Kathy did some guiding. Together they tied flies for the shop and for their clients. In 1985, Jay sold the shop to long-time employee Jimmy Jones, but he continues to teach many of their fly-tying classes. Over the years, Jay has taught entomology classes through the Teton Science School, he has taught the entomology section for many fly-fishing and guide schools, and he has even created a DVD on the subject.

While Jay is a great trout angler, he loves fishing for warm-water species and tying flies for them. Part of this may have to do with his Iowa upbringing. He has done some fun and fascinating work. He is the only person whom I know who has caught walleyes on dry flies—walleyes on top of the water during a *Hexagenia* hatch. He even spent a summer guiding for African tiger fishing on the Zambezi River and developed patterns to catch that species.

Jay has tied flies for himself and others for half a century. Even when he ties a large order, his flies are well tied and consistent. With the Jackson Humpy tradition, Jay and Kathy tied thousands of this pattern. Along with Jack Dennis, they tie them as well as anybody. Their Humpies were the hallmark to match. Jay was the one who added the knotted legs to Dave Whitlock's Dave's Hopper, which is the most common hopper in the world. Technically, it is a Jay–Dave's Hopper. Jay's Rabbit Matukas and Snake River Muddler are effective streamers, and his dun Caddis is a beautiful flat-water pattern. However, one of my favorite

Buchner flies is his diver-headed Dry Stonefly. Popping the fly can wake up docile trout and does a nice job of imitating the motion of a brown stone running on the surface. The pattern is based on some old dry stoneflies fished for Atlantic salmon. Another of Jay's skills is taking an existing pattern and executing it better. His Parachute Hare's Ears and Paradrakes are a step above what you will find in a fly bin.

Jay has contributed to a number of books, including *Fly Tiers Alamanac, Tying with Jack Dennis and Friends,* and *Guide Flies.* He has also published articles in *Fly Fisherman, Fly Tyer,* and *American Angler.* To complement his writing, Jay is an accomplished photographer, which also helps with his entomology presentations.

These days, Jay serves as the coordinator for Team USA for the World Fly-Fishing Championship. He also is the team entomologist and does most of the research on the event's waters, aquatic life, indigenous patterns, and fishing techniques. His experience keeps the young bucks at bay, and he is frequently called upon to cover the team.

I learned a lot from Jay over the years, and it seems like every time that I see him, I learn something new. ◆

Jack Dennis

Jack Dennis Kiwi Muddler

Jack Dennis is one of the biggest influences in my fly-tying and fly-fishing career. Not only have I learned from Jack personally, he has introduced me to many other influential people and has promoted me through his programs, books, videos, and DVDs. He featured me in the video *Understanding Fly Tying Materials* and graciously wrote the foreword to two of my books. I've known Jack for more than twenty years, as both a friend and an employer, and I've fished with him, shot videos, made TV shows, taught clinics, and worked on book projects with him. Along the way, Jack has been a huge help.

Like many others, Jack's *Western Trout Fly Tying Manual, Volume I*, introduced me to tying many of the western trout flies. When I first started tying, I didn't own the book, but I would get it from the library or look at it in a local sporting goods store. I kept trying more and more of the flies in the book. The stories of the flies and fishing information were also helpful to someone who was learning fly tying and fly fishing on their own. In particular, I remember learning to tie Humpies and Royal Humpies from the book. When I was about fourteen, I had purchased a Boots Allen Humpy on a scout trip to Jackson. The fly was functional, but it wasn't a pretty fly.

One summer day, I rode my bike to Zinik's, a local sporting goods chain, and read through the Humpy section of Jack's book. When I saw Jack's Humpies in the book, I immediately noticed how well they were tied. I wanted to tie flies that looked like that. I bought some moose hair and went home to practice tying Humpies. Like any new fly you tie, the first flies were rough, but each one got better. After a couple of days, my Humpies were respectable, and I had a good supply in many different colors. I wanted to try them out, so I rode my bike up City Creek Canyon, near Salt Lake. I went to a pool where I knew I would find fish and sat down to get my gear ready. I noticed a rise and tied on a Humpy. It took a few casts, but I caught a small cutthroat. More fish were now rising and I threw my fly back out. I fished it for awhile to no avail, so I tried another colored Humpy. This worked, but after I caught a fish, the fish became allergic to that color. Over the afternoon, I kept switching Humpy colors, and by doing so I caught about five or six cutthroats, which made me feel good about the flies and my fishing skills.

Years later, I met Jack in person when I worked in his shop. In 1985, I was working for a competing sporting goods store in Jackson, Wyoming. I had a falling out with that establishment and went to look for a new job. My fishing and skiing buddy, John Hanlon, was the floor manager at Jack Dennis Outdoor Shop, so I walked in there and asked him if they needed any help. I started working in the fishing department the next day. A short time later, I started tying Kiwi Muddlers for the shop. This was Jack's fly, and in those days, it wasn't a commercially produced pattern. Jack had tied them in the past for the store, but the time constraints of running a couple of businesses, doing speaking engagements, and raising a family cut into his tying time. Besides in those days of primitive bookkeeping you were paid a dollar a fly out of the till. This was a carrot dangling in front of a flytier's face.

I learned how to tie the Kiwi from the master himself. Jack took me to his office and broke out a vise and some materials. He taught me how to trim the rabbit strip to give it a wide sculpin profile. He also taught me his method of making a Muddler head—by flaring a clump of deer hair on each side of the fly for the head. This distributed the hair more evenly than trying to spin hair around a rough, large base of materials. To this day, this is my preferred method for this technique whether it is on a trout, a bass, or a saltwater fly. That encounter was the start of a great friendship. Tying all those Kiwis affected my streamer concepts and eventually the habitual use of rabbit led to my best-known fly, the Double Bunny.

Kiwi Muddler

Amy Stone, Jack Dennis Kiwi

Jack Dennis was born in Jackson, Wyoming, and from a young age, fishing has been an important part of his life. As a child he spent a good deal of time fishing with his grandfather. One great story from his youth involved using a live mouse to catch a big cutthroat. Jack and his buddies were on Fish Creek and rubber-banded a hook to a mouse. They set the mouse on a piece of wood and floated it down to a deep hole with an overhanging bank. When the stick floated over the hole, they pulled the mouse off, and as it swam, a big cutthroat ate it. However, within a few years Dennis's hair flies were all artificial.

Jack started in the fly-fishing business at the age of twelve, when he sold his first flies, and by age fourteen, he was guiding tourists on local waters. His gregarious personality was well suited to guiding. Boots Allen gave me a great story about a young Jack. Boots left Jack to watch the tackle store while he took a break, and when he came back there wasn't anyone in the store. He looked out the door and saw Jack walking down the street, talking to a customer. He had to finish his fishing story. At age nineteen, he opened his first fishing tackle shop, which has since evolved into the world-famous Jack Dennis Outdoor Shop.

Jack met his wife, Sandy, through a chance encounter. Jack injured himself skiing and was treated in the Jackson hospital by a beautiful, young nurse named Sandy. When they decided to have children, Sandy knew that being a guide would be a difficult job for a family man, so they decided that Jack should expand his guiding and fly business into a full-time shop. Initially, it was only a fly shop, but as time went on, Jack added athletic gear and, in the winter, ski equipment. As it grew, Jack was able to hire solid help and spend more time writing, speaking, and filming.

In 1966, Jack gained national exposure when he did an *American Sportsman* TV show with sports announcer Curt Gowdy, another Wyoming native. In the early 1970s, Jack was writing for some magazines and in 1974 published his first book.

Jack Dennis' Western Trout Fly Tying Manual was the first book to thoroughly cover western-style tying and patterns and set the standard with step-by-step photo instructions. Not only did he give detailed instructions, he also brought the flies and fishing places to life with his stories. In 1980, Jack published his second book, *Western Trout Fly Tying Manual, Volume 2.* The combination of the two *Western Fly Tying Manuals* has sold more than 300,000 copies. In 1995, it was revised with a materials update, a new materials section, and a pattern dictionary, edited by yours truly. In the late 1980s, Jack moved into the video business with *Tying Western Trout Flies*, a hairwing fly video, and *Tying Western Dry Flies*, covering imitative patterns with Mike Lawson. He now has more than twenty fishing and tying videos and DVDs. In 1993, Jack's third book, *Tying Flies with Jack Dennis and Friends*, a compilation of patterns from local friends and those he met through his travels, was published. It included some of the latest innovative patterns by tiers such as Mike Lawson, John Barr, Jay Buchner, Randall Kaufmann, Gary LaFontaine, Guy Turck, Emmett Heath, and myself.

Jack has made a career of teaching seminars and giving programs, and he has it down to a science. Jack will spend six months of the year traveling and doing programs, and those who go to the programs will book him for the next year's event far in advance. Jack is a great storyteller, which is one of the reasons why his programs have been so popular. One time when I did a weekend program with Jack Dennis and Jeff Currier, Jack finished a fly-tying demonstration session without completing the fly. No one cared because the story was so good. While Jack is known for running around ninety miles an hour and sometimes getting projects done at the last minute, once he is on the stage, he has no parallel. For twelve years, Jack, the late Gary LaFontaine, and Mike Lawson did seminars as the Traveling Fly Fisherman, also nicknamed the Three Amigos. Alone they were very good, but together, they were outstanding. The program ended with Gary LaFontaine's illness and consequent death in 2002.

Jack is an international promoter of fly fishing, and in 1989, he organized a fishing summit between the United States secretary of state and the Russian ambassador, Eduard Shevardnadze, as a way

Jack Dennis

(tied by Jack Dennis)

BLEEDING HEART KIWI

Hook – TMC 5263 3XL Streamer #10 – #2

Thread – Red A

Underbody – Lead wire

Tail – Frayed ends of mylar body

Body – Pearl mylar tubing

Rib – Red wire

Underwing – Tuft of red orange rabbit fur

Wing – Cottontail magnum rabbit strip cut to diamond shape

Overwing – Multi-color Krystal Flash

Collar & head – Natural, olive and red deer hair

AMY STONE

Amy Special

Hook – TMC 200 3XL natural bend, sizes #16 – #8

Yellow – 8/0

Underbody – Yellow foam

Tag – Orange Antron or rabbit

Abdomen – Pale yellow dubbing

Underwing – Pearl Rainbow Thread

Post – butts of underwing

Wing – Light elk

Thorax – Pale yellow dubbing

Hackle – Light dun

to promote friendship and relaxation while tackling international diplomacy. For his work in promoting fly fishing, in 2001 the Federation of Fly Fishers gave him the FFF Ambassadors Award. Jack has been a fly-fishing tourism advisor to the governments of New Zealand, Australia, Chile, and Argentina, and to many western U.S. states. In 1993, *United Airlines* magazine named him as one of the best known and influential Wyoming-born personalities. Over the years, Jack has also worked as a professional consultant and promoter for many of the premier fly-fishing companies.

Jack has been involved in many different fly-fishing competition venues. He was a member of the Trout Unlimited team for the Russia–United States Angling Games and of the U.S. team for the World Fly Fishing Championships in 1988 and 1991. In 1997, he was on the organizing committee for the seventeenth World Championship held in Jackson and, for a few years, has been the coach of Team USA. However, Jack's most important competition is the Jackson Hole One Fly. This competition is different than most, since conservation moneys and camaraderie are the most important parts of the event. The One Fly is the brainchild of Jack, Curt Gowdy, Paul Brunn, and Dan Abrams, who believed that a contest on the Snake River promoting catch-and-release fishing would be good for the sport and fisheries. The contest came to fruition in September 1986, with regional anglers competing, but in the last twenty years, it has become an international event. The One Fly has led the way in stream improvements, both monetarily and politically, and has donated more than $650,000 to conservation projects.

Jack Dennis is a busy man, but he has taken the time to influence and help me. Many thanks to a good friend. ◆

GEORGE GRANT

Grant Black Creeper

Growing up in the West, I have known of George Grant's flies for many years. In fact, George and his flies were often referred to in mystical reverence. These were the stonefly imitations to try and tie or adapt to your needs. He influenced my fly tying by setting a tradition for western fly tying and creating a fly-fishing and fly-tying climate for those who followed. His woven stonefly nymphs are not only pieces of art, they are significant steps in the evolution toward imitative western flies and consequently the modern flies we fish. His books have preserved an important history of influential western flies, tiers, and tying methods, and by doing so, they have created a link to the past and a foundation for the future.

While attending events sponsored by the Federation of Fly Fishers, I met Todd Collins, George's protégé. Todd and I had a great time watching each other tie and talking fishing and tying, and we soon became good friends. Todd has an extensive knowledge of historical Montana fly patterns, and he frequently teaches a Grant fly-tying class. With his help, I was able to see the Grant methods and flies in person and learn their history. I'm greatly indebted to Todd. Todd has followed in George's footsteps in conservation as well, and has been president of the Big Hole River Foundation. He also has tied many of the Grant patterns that have been used to raise money for the foundation.

For the better part of a century, George Grant has been tying his productive hair hackle patterns and protecting Montana's waters, creating an unmatched legacy. George was a conservationist before conservation was popular, and through his influence and writings, he has brought others to the cause of protecting Montana waters. George did this in Butte, Montana, an area known more for its extensive mining than its environmental attitudes. As early as 1933, George was practicing catch and release. His hair hackled patterns and tying techniques were revolutionary and are now an important part of Montana history. Because of his writings, another generation can carry on this tradition of fly tying and conservation.

George grew up in Butte, Montana, and according to George, he was the runt of the litter. Consequently, his parents didn't see him becoming a mine laborer. He was therefore encouraged to take high school courses in writing, journalism, bookkeeping, and typing. Later on, these skills proved vital to his conservation, educational, and historical pursuits. After high school, he furthered his education at a business college, and worked as a personal secretary, performed various clerical jobs, and had a job with the railroad. He started fly fishing before he was out of high school, but without a car, he was limited to times when he could get a ride to the water.

He started fishing the Big Hole River in 1925 and was immediately addicted to it. In 1928, he became interested in fly tying, a hobby he pursued well into his nineties. To learn about fly tying, he read the Herter's catalogs and dissected flies from famous Montana tiers such as Jack Boehme, Bill Beaty, and Franz Pott. He was especially fascinated by the Pott flies. He liked the way they fished and admired their durability. At the time, the Sandy Mite was one of the most popular and effective flies. It took a while to figure out how Pott braided the hair hackle, but George deciphered it and came up with a better method. Pott's hair hackle technique was patented, but George applied for a patent on his modified method and was granted patent 2,178,031 in 1939. He went on to create a number of woven hackle flies, including wets, streamers, and dries. Among the most popular were his Creeper and Hellgrammite patterns, which imitated many of the stonefly nymphs found on the Big Hole River. He used pins lashed to the sides of the

Black Creeper, Featherback

Black Creeper

hook shank to give these flies wide bodies like the natural, and he was the first to use monofilament as an overbody on his flies. This made them durable and added segmentation and depth to the flies.

In 1933, George lost his job with the Union Pacific Railroad, and instead of transferring to Salt Lake City, he stayed in Montana so that he would be close to his beloved Big Hole River. He rented a cabin in Dewey on the Big Hole, and fished almost everyday except for when he worked odd jobs. In 1937, he started tying commercially and did this until 1951. At different

Grant

BLACK CREEPER (tied by George Grant)

Hook – Mustad 9492 size 7
Thread – Black Nymo "A"
Underbody – Brass pins and black wool
Body – 25# black oval monofilament
Belly strip – Orange floss
Hackle – Black .005 Tynex fibers (nylon brush filaments)

times, he had fly shops in West Yellowstone and Butte. Later on, he worked for Treasure State Sporting Goods, a large wholesale and retail sporting goods operation.

With an extensive knowledge of Montana waters, George knew that the rivers needed protection in order to maintain and improve the fisheries and their surroundings. George attacked this pursuit as vigorously as he did his fishing and tying. After George retired from commercial tying, he tied flies for donations. These flies and shadow boxes brought thousands of dollars for conservation purposes. He wrote and distributed the *River Rat,* Montana Trout Unlimited's newsletter, and through this publication he was able to get people across the country to contribute to conservation projects in Montana. *Grant's Riffle,* a compilation of the *River Rat* articles, is now sold by the Big Hole River Foundation as a fundraiser. George was given the Art Gingrich Memorial Life membership by the FFF for his work on the *River Rat.*He butted heads with politicians and many times came out the winner. He protects the Big Hole River like a parent takes care of his or her child, and when Reichle Dam was proposed to be built on the river between Melrose and Twin Bridges, he fought it tooth and nail. It would have inundated over ten miles of his favorite river. Due to his efforts, the dam is a story and not a reality. In 1989, George was instrumental in creating the Big Hole River Foundation. Because of George's influence, catch and release, special regulations, and streambed preservation are commonplace, and state governments see the economic significance of recreational fishing. In 1973, he was awarded the Buz Buzek Award by the FFF for his contribution to fly tying. His books *The Art of Weaving Hair Hackles* and *Montana Trout Flies* pass the flies of another time onto the future, and they include illustrations by the author.

George passed away on November 2, 2008, at the age of 102. Not many live more than a century, and even fewer have had as much influence on conservation and tying for such a long time. ◆

THE HARROPS

Harrop Hairwing Dun

MOST FLY-FISHING FAMILIES WOULD BE ECSTATIC to have one flytier of the Harrops' stature, but in this family, they have four. Rene, Bonnie, Shayne, and Leslie tie great numbers of flies, and of a quality most tiers work a lifetime to achieve. The beauty of their flies lies in the surprisingly simple design and in the perfect execution. As opposed to most famous tiers, their flies can purchased by the non-collector. The Harrops are definitely the first family of spring-creek flies, and the House of Harrop is a regal entity.

Many of the Harrops' flies and ideas have found their way into my flies, but it was Rene's Hairwing Dun that had the biggest impact. Jeff Currier showed me the fly and mentioned that he had caught some nice fish on the Henry's Fork with it. When I first saw the pattern, I knew it would work. The wing angled back more than in a traditional mayfly pattern, but real mayflies don't have wings that extend ninety degrees from their body. I quickly went to tying some Pale Morning Hairwing Duns (PMDs). I caught fish on the Henry's Fork and soon afterward was fishing the South Fork. Early July on the South Fork brings out salmon flies, golden stones, the smaller yellow sallies, and PMDs. As the big stones taper off, the sallies and PMDs become summer's dominant hatches. Fish can get keyed in on either one of them, and this seems to be caused by which hatch predominates on that bank or riffle. Instead of switching flies while boat fishing, I just lifted the wing for a PMD and smashed it down for a sally. It worked on the fish, and a short time later, I borrowed this concept for my Everything Emerger. Later on, I learned that Rene's fly had evolved through necessity from a Troth Elk-Hair Caddis. I guess this goes to show that evolution never ends.

All of the Harrops grew up in St. Anthony, Idaho, near the fabled waters of the Henry's Fork, and their time is split between summers in Last Chance and winters in St. Anthony. Rene started tying flies for himself in 1954. At the time, if you didn't have money, you had to tie flies if you wanted to fly-fish. The economics of youth required it, and through a lack of funds, the world was presented with a family of world-class tiers. During the 1950s in eastern Idaho, instruction was non-existent, and Rene learned to tie flies by dissecting the flies that he bought. Rene didn't see many good fly tiers until the mid 1960s. In 1968, his tying evolved to commercial production.

Rene went to Rick's College to play football, and along the way, he took some art classes, which proved valuable later on. In 1966, he married Bonnie. Both loved to be on the water, and Rene taught Bonnie to tie flies. During the mid 1970s, he started writing articles for magazines and needed illustrations to complement them. Rene decided to do the illustrations himself and went back to his art training. Since then, his art has grown and expanded to be a self-supporting entity. Rene's art is complemented by Bonnie's beautiful framing.

In 1976, Rene and Bonnie started Henry's Fork Anglers in Last Chance along with Mike and Sheralee Lawson, also icons of spring-creek tying and fishing. Business was much more seasonable than it is today, and fly-fishing tourism wasn't at the same level as it is now. In the best-case scenario, it was a tough venture, and both families had small children to support. Because of economics, they separated in 1977—the Lawsons doing the shop and the Harrops taking the fly-tying business.

Important influences for the Harrops were Doug Swisher and Carl Richards. Their book, *Selective Trout*, was published in 1971, and it was one of the first books that explored imitations of aquatic flies at all levels of development. Their patterns and ideas were important predecessors to the Harrops' fly ideas. The Harrops tied flies for their shop, and while Swisher and Richards created the patterns, the Harrops perfected them.

Hairwing Dun – Pale Morning Dun

Hairwing Dun – Green Drake

Shane and Leslie started tying flies and fly fishing at a young age, and they continue their parents' tradition of excellence. By high school, they were an important part of the House of Harrop. As Maggie Merriman comments, "It's in their genes."

The Harrops were among the first American tiers to use cul de canard (CDC) and played a significant role in the acceptance of the material in the United States. According to Rene, they are still finding ways to use it. They were also pioneers in using biot bodies. Biot bodies form a smooth, sparse, segmented body, which can prove critical in fooling tough fish. Because of

Harrop

HARROP HAIRWING DUN – GREEN DRAKE (tied by Shayne Harrop)

Hook – Standard dry fly, sizes 12 -14
Thread – Olive 8/0
Tail – Dark dun hackle fibers
Abdomen – Olive dyed turkey biot
Thorax – Olive dubbing
Hackle – Olive dyed grizzly
Wing – Dyed black elk hair

the Harrops, turkey biots are now a common tying material. They have even used trimmed biot as wings on some of their patterns. At different times, the Harrops have had a mail-order supply business, but with their partnership in Trouthunter, they moved that part of the business to the shop so that they could spend their time tying.

While the Harrops still provide flies to lucky individuals and shops, they have been contract tiers for many years. They first worked with Umpqua Feather Merchants and are now aligned with Solitude Flies. Some of their best-known flies are Captive Duns, Transitional Duns, CDC Caddis, Biot Slow-Water Caddis, Hairwing Duns, CDC Biot Spinners, and Last Chance Cripples. Along with the Lawsons, they are among the few who can tie a perfect No Hackle. Although their flies are innovative, Rene still ties on an old Thompson Model A vise as well as a discontinued Thompson model and would be in a bad way if he lost his outdated Thompson whip finisher.

The Harrops are famous in Japan, and in the 1990s, Rene designed fishing gear to be licensed under his name. The Japanese tiers enjoy perfection in their fly tying, and the Harrops provide it.

To protect their favorite fishery, the Harrops were founding members of the Henry's Fork Foundation. This group is at the leading edge of conservation and provides solutions that benefit fishery and agricultural needs.

The Harrops continue to produce innovative, immaculate, and simple flies that first catch fish and that always catch fishermen. ◆

GEORGE HERTER

Herter Spey

GEORGE LEONARD HERTER'S FLY IDEAS were way ahead of their time, and through marketing they found their way into my flies and the flies of many others. For many flytiers my age or older, *Herter's Catalog* was an important source of fly-tying tools, materials, and instruction, and the man behind this was George Herter. Even fly-tying legends like Dan Bailey sourced some materials from Herter's vast selection. My first fly-tying kit and tools came from Herter's, and my first fly-tying book, *Professional Fly Tying, Spinning and Tackle Making,* was written by George Herter. Herter helped start myself and others down the slippery path of fly tying.

The *Herter's Catalog* was an outdoor tradition for years. Herter was a clever entrepreneur. He charged you three dollars for his catalog, but he gave that back on your initial order. The vast catalog had every outdoor item you could think of, and the product captions and stories were great. George had the best of everything—just ask him. For me, reading the *Herter's Catalog* was a great sportsman's journey traveling around the world, hunting and fishing in remote places for exotic creatures. It whetted my appetite for outdoor adventure and gave me dreams of catching Arctic char and pike on a remote northern Canadian lake and then turning around and shooting a polar bear—and, of course, skinning it with my Herter's Ulu knife. This was the ultimate in armchair angling and hunting. Oh, the days of daydreaming adventure—may they never die.

My brother-in-law, John Wightman, was my scoutmaster and had some fly-tying stuff from his Boy Scout days. I've fished for as long as I can remember, so tying flies seemed like a logical choice. John dusted off an old box of tying tools with a few materials and we tried to make some flies. John was rusty and I was inexperienced, but I saw the potential for fun and wanted to try it some more. I looked in a *Herter's Catalog* that he had and found a basic tying kit. It took a while, but I saved my money, and my sister, Julie, sent a check to Herter's for a fly-tying kit and some extra materials. I'm greatly indebted. Once I had the kit and book, I saved my money and ordered other materials to tie new flies. This was long before the age of credit cards and the Internet; it was the era of true mail order. Mail in a check, and they would mail the product.

In the kit was the book *Professional Fly Tying, Spinning and Tackle Making*, written and illustrated by George Herter. It was the first book that I owned on fly tying, and my initial tying endeavors followed the instructions and pattern recipes in the manual. His method of snipping fibers off the base of a hackle stem to help the thread secure is part of my everyday fly tying. I'm glad that I learned from this book, because George had an uninhibited view of fly tying, and I learned about using non-traditional materials. This was the start of my use of odd materials, which continues today.

George's flies were way before their time. They pushed the envelope and gave my young mind a bunch of different concepts that I might not have learned otherwise. Long before foam was a standard item, George incorporated Kapok into his dry flies for floatability. Kapok is a buoyant natural fiber that was used in life jackets for many years. What would have happened if George had closed-cell foam? Herter was an early promoter of marabou, and this influenced my use of mobile materials in flies. He used marabou on streamer patterns, of course, but he also put it into dry flies, such as his Chateaubriand and Herter Composite. This gave a natural motion to the floaters, and this was in the recesses of my mind when I came up with the early Convertibles.

George Herter's background as both a fly fisherman and lure fisherman helped him form his broad range of ideas, and no doubt as an extensive traveler, he was able to pick up tidbits from other places and

Spey Fly

try concepts on a variety of species. He was one of the first I can remember to try to duplicate lure actions into flies. He had a classic "Rapala" fly with a carp scale lip on it, and his Spey Fly streamer used rubber strands for the wing and hackle on the fly. He had a series of match-the-hatch streamers long before that became a modern concept.

Much of my early knowledge of fly patterns came from the pages of Herter's book. Pattern descriptions weren't just recipes, but the history of the fly, the creator, and what the fly was used for. Even for those who don't tie,

Herter

SPEY FLY (tied by Scott Sanchez)

Hook – 4XL streamer, size 2 – 8
Thread – Black 3/0
Tail – Three strands of black rubber
Body – white chenille
Rib – Gold tinsel
Wing – Six strands of red rubber
Throat – six strands of grey rubber
Eyes – flat plastic eyes

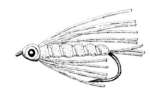

the book is a wonderful history lesson. Of course, George's overtly biased opinions of flies were part of the book's flavor. George's black-and-white illustrations and drawn color plates showed the flies. This was in the days before cheap digital color separations and was a classic look of many of the fishing books of the era. George also wrote a number of other books, including the *Professional Guides Manual; Professional Loading of Rifle, Pistol and Shotgun Cartridges; West Coast Fly and Streamer Patterns; How to Get Out of the Rat Race and Live on $10 a Month;* and *Secret Fresh and Saltwater Fishing Tricks of the Fifty Best Professional Fishermen.* George was a prolific writer and marketer.

Unfortunately, I don't have my original Herter's tying manual, but when I worked at the Austin Angler, they had a used-book section. I found a copy of *Herter's Minnows of North America and Their Streamer Imitations.* Not only did this book have George's match-the-hatch streamer imitations, it also included the pattern dictionary from *Professional Fly Tying, Spinning and Tackle Making.*

It's good to have an old companion back, and one of Herter's patterns just might surface in one of my new flies. ◆

RANDALL KAUFMANN

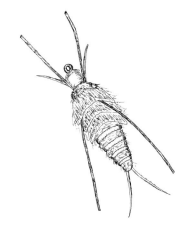

Kaufmann Stone

RANDALL KAUFMANN HAS INFLUENCED MY FLY TYING through his books, fly patterns, and our conversations. Flies like his Stimulator and the Kaufmann Stone are standards and are the basis for some of my flies and for those of others. His nymph-tying books taught me about a wide variety of nymphs and their imitations and purposes, and his dry-fly and bonefish books have given me valuable insights. It is hard to imagine the modern world of fly fishing without Randall Kaufmann.

I've been fortunate to have met Randall and fish with him on a number of occasions. Jack Dennis and Randall are long-time friends, and in July 1991, Jack asked me if I wanted to take Randall fishing. I had briefly met Randall on different occasions, and I own a couple of his books and certainly had looked at others. Randall enjoys hiking the backcountry, so we traveled into the Bechler River near the southwestern corner of Yellowstone National Park. We had a great time on the trip talking about flies and fly fishing and exchanging ideas and observations. The hike was enjoyable, and to top off the day, we had some excellent hopper fishing. When you are around Randall, there is no doubt that he enjoys the fishing and savors the entire fishing experience. A glimpse at the photos in his books makes you realize that he takes time to smell the flowers and soak in the vistas, and when you fish with him, this is undeniable. Other ventures have taken us on boat and foot to various blue-ribbon waters of Wyoming, Montana, and Yellowstone National Park. We've had some good fishing and good chats, and each time has been a learning experience.

Randall's well-thought-out books are not only valuable tying manuals, they also teach the history of the flies and how and where to fish them. The material sections are also helpful, since the fly will only be as good its components. Over the years, as printing technologies have advanced, Randall has updated his books with the most recent information and appearance. The books have made my tying more productive and enjoyable.

Randall grew up in California. At the age of fourteen, he was introduced to fly fishing and tying by his stepfather, Jack Moore. Randall's interest in angling was cultivated through family vacations, which included trips to western mountains. When he was fifteen, they would drive from their home in Rialto, California, and sell flies along the eastern slope of the Sierras at Bishop, Mammoth Lakes, and June Lake. Through his tying sales, he was able to accumulate enough money to buy backpacking gear. Prior to having a car, his mother, Oda, would drive him around to sell his flies and drop him off on fishing and backpacking trips. As he saved more tying money, he bought a car, and winters were spent fly tying, which enabled summer travel and the necessary gear.

Soon his adventures went further and took more time. Backpacking in Wyoming's Wind River Range became one of his favorites. While on a summer break from high school, Randall and his younger brother, Lance, ran into Jack Dennis at his father's Lander, Wyoming, liquor and sporting goods store. Jack was tying a big order of Irresistibles. The Kaufmanns helped him finish the order and in turn learned how to tie hair flies. Afterward, they went backpacking and fishing in the Winds. A lifelong friendship was started among two of the world's most prolific tiers.

The appearance of Dennis Black was to become a significant event in Randall's life. In 1966, Dennis Black, a California commercial tier, went to the Federation of Fly Fishers conclave, which was held at Jackson Lake Lodge in Grand Teton National Park, Wyoming. While he was there, he went into the Rod and Reel Shop in Jackson and noticed two flytiers in the back. They were Randall Kaufmann and Jack Dennis. The three struck up a conversation, and Randall, Jack, and Dennis spent a few days fishing

Golden Stone Stimulator (top), Kaufmann Golden Stone Nymph

Kaufmann Golden Stone Nymph

and tying. At the time, Randall was facing the prospect of having to get a college diploma and a real job. Dennis was wholesaling flies to Orvis and other operations, and he needed more tying capacity. He talked Jack and Randall into tying for him. Randall took an order for 600 dozen flies at $1.80 a dozen, with a six-week deadline. The order was completed and he received a check for $1,000. This amount was far more valuable than it would be now, and at the age of nineteen, Randall decided that he should expand his tying and make more money. The idea of getting a real job disappeared. Randall's relationship with Dennis Black proved to be very important for both men.

I've heard stories from Jack about a speed-tying contest between Randall, Jack, and Dennis. This group, with a mix of other young trout bums, ran around the Greater Yellowstone area chasing trout, girls, and cocktails, and not always in that order. Boys will be boys. They floated rivers, waded streams, and explored the backcountry—all the while commercially tying flies to fund their lifestyle.

In 1968, Dennis Black moved to Winchester, Oregon, and started a mail-order fly shop on the banks of the Umpqua River, which eventually evolved into Umpqua Feather Merchants. Meanwhile, Randall went to college at the Banff School of Fine Arts in Canada. In 1969, Randall visited Dennis on a trip home from school, and shortly afterward he moved to Oregon. Randall helped Dennis with his production tying, and together they worked to develop more efficient ways to produce flies. Dennis was instrumental in giving Randall and Lance the confidence to start their own fly-fishing business.

In 1971, Randall and Lance, along with their parents, Jack and Oda, started Streamborn Flies. The mail-order business originated in their parents' garage in Tigard, Oregon, near Portland. They sent out catalogs, and soon the business outgrew the garage. A storefront was added along with regular hours. Oda did the accounting, and kept the boys in check. Over the years, stores in Seattle and Bellevue, Washington, were added.

In 1972, Dennis Black started Umpqua Feather Merchants and its contract tier program. This was the first fly-tying business to pay a royalty to the tier for his or her patterns. Other flies had been produced overseas, with the primary intent of keeping the price reasonable, but Dennis was interested in having premium imported flies. Initially there was skepticism in the fly-fishing market, but as the flies came to the United States, they were met with approval. Randall was one of the first contract tiers, and he was instrumental in building their program into its premium stature. Randall's name and patterns made the fly program marketable and helped to build interest among shops and tiers. Royalties from this program have helped Randall to pursue his tying and writing career. He is also one of the reasons why Tiemco hooks are so popular.

In the early 1970s, Randall met Frank Amato, who published regional fishing magazines and books. In 1975, the Portland, Oregon, publisher printed Randall's first book, *American Nymph Tying Manual*. This book brought nymph tying and fishing to the forefront. The book included practical tying information, detailed tying photos, and the history of many effective flies. This book was the start of a prolific writing career. This classic book is still in print today.

In 1984, Randall and Ron Cordes coauthored *Lake Fishing With a Fly*. This is considered the definitive American book on the subject, and it expanded Randall's repertoire beyond fly tying into angling instruction. Mike Stidham's illustrations were used in this book and became standard in later books. Like his first book, it was published by Amato Publications.

In 1986, Randall moved into self-publishing with *The Fly Tyers Nymph Manual*, an updated and expanded version of his *American Nymph Tying Manual*. This was done under the Western Fisherman's Press label. While the original book put him on the map, *The Fly Tyers Nymph Manual* elevated his writing popularity to a new level. This book and the three revisions, called *Tying Nymphs*, have become the bibles for nymph tiers and are standard reference books for most tiers and anglers. They brought the importance of underwater imitations to many anglers and were the building blocks for modern nymph-fishing and

KAUFMANN GOLDEN STONE NYMPH

Hook – Tiemco 5263RBL size 6 – 8
Bead – Gold tungsten
Weight – Size .025–.035 lead-free wire smashed flat
Thread – Black 6/0
Tail – Brown turkey biot
Rib – Amber V-rib
Abdomen – Kaufmann golden stone mix
Wingcase – Natural brown turkey tail treated with Flexament,
           3 sections trimmed to V
Thorax – Kaufmann golden stone mix
Legs – Black round rubber
Antennae – Brown turkey biot

Kaufmann

(tied by Randall Kaufmann)

GOLDEN STONE (*Acroneuria*) STIMULATOR

Hook – 200RBL, SIZE 6 – 10
Thread – Fl fire orange
Tail – Golden deer and medium natural elk mixed
Rib – Gold wire
Body – Kaufmann golden stone mix
Hackle – Furnace or dun
Flash – Gold and pearl Krystal flash and pearl Mirror Flash
Underwing – Grey Web Wing
Overwing – Golden deer and medium natural elk mixed, spread wide
Legs – Black round medium rubber
Hackle – Grizzly saddle
Thorax – Kaufmann Stimulator thorax mix and peacock

fly patterns. A wealth of information explains materials, tools, and techniques. Randall's photographic skills also played an important role in his books by showing techniques. In addition, fly histories and well-thought-out stories added character and life to the fly patterns. Over the years, many tiers have learned how to tie their first fly from this book.

Self-publishing was important to later books and revisions, and it gave Randall control of the editorial content and the option to update when desired. In this way, he could modernize good information with revisions and take advantage of printing innovations. Changes in printing options have allowed him to change black-and-white instructions to color, and his use of color fly-tying steps has pushed others to follow suit.

In 1991, Kaufmann's *Tying Dry Flies* was published, and the dry-fly counterpart to Randall's nymph books became another mandatory fly-tying text. Randall's excellent writing now covered most trout flies. This book gave in-depth technical information while maintaining the enjoyable ambience of fly fishing. The 1995 and 2002 revisions contained additional information and color tying steps.

Through Kaufmann's Fly Fishing Expeditions, Randall was able to develop a passion for bonefishing. He was able to visit numerous saltwater flats around the world, and his inquisitive mind figured out ways to catch bonefish and how to explain the technique to others. This wealth of information was put into his 1992 book, *Bonefish With A Fly*. In 2000, he published *Bonefishing!* an updated and full-color revised version. It includes hundreds of Brian OKeefe's exceptional photos and Mike Stidham's artwork. The information is presented in a solid but informal way that puts you in the situation and guides you through it.

In 1995, Randall authored *Fly Patterns of Umpqua Feather Merchants*. This book featured a compilation of patterns from Umpqua's contract tiers, along with chapters from some of the preeminent tiers and a history of the operation. It is a great pattern encyclopedia and includes more than a thousand flies. An expanded second edition was published in 1998.

Most authors would be happy with books of this stature, but Randall kept improving his. Although many beginners have learned to tie from his books, in 2002, he came out with a more general beginner book, *Fly Tying Made Easy for Beginners*. In this text, he covered a variety of nymphs, emergers, dries, streamers, and steelhead flies. A smaller, less expensive variation, *Fly Tying for Beginners,* is also available, and it is a perfect companion for entry-level fly-tying kits.

Randall's books are standards. His approach to step-by-step tying with excellent photos has taught many tiers to tie without hands-on instruction. His books do one of the most important things in teaching—they don't assume that people know something. They cover tying in a thorough, logical manner.

Randall has promoted conservation through his writing and his flies. He has been instrumental in making barbless hooks standard and has encouraged proper fish handling. His royalty patterns from Umpqua are sold with barbless hooks. He suggests using plated hooks on his saltwater flies, and he advocates the use of non-lead weights on flies whenever feasible. His books cover how to release and photograph fish with a minimal effect on them. This is very important, because many well-meaning anglers kill fish with their cameras.

Randall Kaufmann has been an important part of fly tying and fly fishing for more than thirty years. His writing, ideas, and fly patterns have brought much enjoyment to many anglers. ◆

Bernard "Lefty" Kreh

Lefty Deceiver

Lefty may not have been the first to saltwater fly-fish, but he is certainly one of the foremost. He introduced a couple of generations to saltwater fly fishing, and his books and articles gave a wealth of knowledge to a landlocked Wyoming boy. The classic *Fly Fishing in Salt Water* is the bible of the sport, and his *Salt Water Fly Patterns* books showed me the range of fly patterns being tied around the world. This, in turn, gave me many ideas on how to create and modify patterns. Lefty's Deceiver, a fifty-year-old fly, is still as effective today as it was when it was originated and is probably the most widely fished and copied fly in salt water. Lefty not only has a vast knowledge, he has a great way of simplifying and teaching. He doesn't complicate when it is not needed, and he breaks down his explanations into digestible pieces. He has knowledge without the ego, and he seems like a surrogate father to the novice.

In recent years, saltwater tying has been a major catalyst in flies and fly materials. Salt water to a large degree has accelerated the use of synthetics, and this has also flowed over into trout flies. Probably the biggest influence has been in streamer and bait-fish imitations; however, methods gleaned from the salt can even be found in spring-creek patterns. Lefty's knowledge, articles, and books helped speed along these welcome advancements.

The first Lefty Kreh book that I owned was *Fishing the Flats*, which he coauthored with Mark Sosin. I hadn't been saltwater fly fishing yet, but I knew that a trip would be on the horizon. When the revised edition of *Fly Fishing in Salt Water* was published, I bought that as well. I learned a lot from those books, and they stirred my interest. I also found out which flies to tie from Lefty's book and went on a rampage tying them. Tying saltwater flies was great. I learned about epoxy, hot glue, and different ways to incorporate materials. It is always fun to try new things, and the world of salt water wasn't encumbered by the piousness of trout tying. You were encouraged to get wild. With many trout flies, you tie them and they go in a box with barely a glance. With saltwater flies, you have a friend to talk to and pet, and you can look into its eyes. I went nuts and soon had more saltwater flies than you could ever fish, but I kept tying. Tying these flies also made me think about how I could incorporate some of the materials techniques into my trout flies. When I went on my first saltwater trip to Belize in January 1988, I had the chance to use the knowledge and flies gleaned from Lefty's books. I had a great time, Lefty's methods worked, and I added a new fishing addiction. Also on that trip, the idea that became the Double Bunny was formed.

I had the opportunity to meet Lefty in August 1988, when the national Trout Unlimited banquet was held in Jackson. For that event, I tied a big box of saltwater flies as a donation. There were mostly flats flies, Charlies, small epoxies, and some of my own Bunny Crabs. Lefty was in the process of collecting flies for his upcoming saltwater fly pattern book, which was being done in conjunction with Marriot's Fly Shop. He noticed the flies, and through Jack Dennis and Paul Brunn, he found out who I was. One night that week, Jack Dennis invited me to dinner with a group of people. We had dinner at the Wort Hotel with Lefty, Jack Dennis, Jimmy Nix, and a couple of other people. Lefty was nonstop with jokes and comments. I got a chance to talk to him for a while, and he asked me to send some flies and recipes for a few of my flies. He gave me one of his Deceivers. When the book came out, I was excited to see my fly in it. I was pleasantly surprised when I saw my crab as one of the patterns on the cover. This was the first time one of my flies had been covered in a major publication, and eventually, this small start led to a career in writing.

Olive/White Lefty's Deceiver

The *Salt Water Fly Patterns* book pushed me to tie even more saltwater flies, and tying clients who bought the book had me tie some of the flies they saw in its pages. Living in Wyoming, I tied a lot of saltwater flies but didn't get to fish them in the salt every day, but still, tying the flies kept expanding my knowledge and I started thinking more about bait-fish patterns in general—how to improve the patterns and fish them better. Fish on the Snake, Salt, Green, and South Fork rivers came into contact with salinity, and my flies went on saltwater trips with others as well. The large eyes on bait-fish patterns are an idea that I picked up from Lefty. Plenty of saltwater flies were tried on trout, and they ate them.

Lefty is an angler with a wide range of experience—he has fished everywhere for everything. He is like a giant encyclopedia of fishing. He is at home on a small trout stream, a small-mouth river, or in blue water. Lefty is an equipment tinkerer working on projects to make fishing easier and less frustrating. His little tricks are huge. Tips like cooking shock tippet mono to straighten it and then putting it into a tube to keep it that way don't seem important until you are rushing to rig up flies for big fish. Now, pre-straightened shock tippet and built leaders are sold commercially. Lefty's tricks for sharpening hooks, making epoxy flies, and pre-rigging class tippets on a spool help out immensely.

His photographic skills also complement his written instruction. He uses photos in a way that illustrates the ideas. His photography skills happen to expand beyond fly fishing. His L.L. Bean book of photography is great for the outdoor photographer looking for useful and practical information. It's like Lefty's fishing books with classic homemade devices designed to simplify tasks. I learned a few tricks from it that improved my photography.

Lefty was born and raised in Frederick, Maryland, and started fishing at a young age as both a form of recreation and a source of food. Growing up during the Depression was tough for anyone, but when his father passed away, things were even tougher. Fishing was a pastime to which he and his younger brother could walk. He spent some time in Europe during World War II, but when he came back, he was back to fishing the area's waters. He had a great reputation as a smallmouth bass expert, and in 1947, Joe Brooks, who was a regional writer at the time, had Lefty take him fishing on the Potomac. It was a windy day and Joe pulled out a fly rod. Lefty asked him if he wanted to use a casting rod instead. Joe said that casting a fly rod in the wind wasn't a problem. That day, Joe went on to outfish Lefty with his fly rod. Lefty was impressed. Outfishing a good angler on his or her home water usually doesn't happen. The next day, Lefty drove fifty miles to have Joe give him a casting lesson and buy a rod. His fly career had started. Lefty soon found out that the further you could cast, the more fish you could fool, and he lengthened his casting stroke to accomplish this. This was considered heresy in the proper world of fly fishing, but it worked and was the beginning of the modern casting style.

With his reputation as an outdoor expert, Lefty started writing for the Frederick newspaper in 1951, and within a few years he was contributing to four papers. This was in addition to working for the federal government's Biological Warfare Unit. He worked the night shift so that he could fish during the day. Lefty met a newspaper editor who was using a thirty-five-millimeter camera, which was fairly new at the time, and much more portable than the status-quo gear. He learned how to use the thirty-five-millimeter camera, documented his adventures, and used it to illustrate his articles. This gave him a huge edge over other writers. The norm was that an editor received the text from the writer and then hired an artist to illustrate the piece. With Lefty's one-stop shopping, magazines loved him. Soon he had too much work. Lefty has made a career of covering topics with which he is intimately familiar, and that list is pretty extensive. Books are the other part of his writing prowess, and he has authored twenty-nine knowledge-filled books on fishing, casting, flyfishing, and photography.

The Lefty's Deceiver came about in the late 1950s as an improvement on the streamers of the day. The standard bait-fish patterns were tied with chenille bodies and feather or hair wings. Their profile was

Kreh

OLIVE WHITE LEFTY'S DECEIVER (tied by Lefty Kreh)

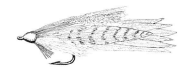

Hook – Standard saltwater, sizes 6/0 – 4

Thread – White 3/0

Tail – Long white saddle hackle with olive dyed grizzly saddle hackle on the sides and silver Flashabou

Body – White chenille

Collar – White bucktail

Topping – Olive dyed grizzly saddle hackle, olive Flashabou and peacock herl

Throat – Red Flashabou

Head – Red Flashabou coated with cement

small and they were prone to foul. On a striper trip to Chesapeake Bay, he came up with the idea for the Deceiver. It cast well, had a big profile, and didn't foul. Best of all, the fish liked it. The original was tied in all white, but other colors were soon added. In the mid 1960s, Mylar became available and Lefty added this icing to an already very good cake.

Lefty spent eleven years in Florida, and through this learned numerous techniques to add to his arsenal. The 1960s and 1970s were the golden age in the Florida Keys, with numerous unpressured fish and vast areas to fish for them. Most of the saltwater techniques and tackle we take for granted now were developed in this time and place. Lefty worked at various Florida papers as an outdoor columnist, and while he was at the *Miami Herald,* he ran the MET fishing tournament. This was the biggest tournament in the world, and through it he met everyone. With his casting abilities, he was in demand for casting lessons and taught many of today's big names how to cast further and more effectively. In turn, through contact with many of the better guides and anglers, he was given a master's degree in light-tackle saltwater fishing. Eventually, he moved back home to Maryland and became the outdoor writer for the *Baltimore Sun* newspapers. Lefty is now eighty-three, and as he says, "I've failed retirement horribly." I'm glad he continues to add to my instruction.

For his knowledge and the ability to teach others, Lefty has received numerous awards, including the Lifetime Achievement Award from the American Sportsfishing Association, the Lifetime Contribution Award from North American Fly Tackle Trade Association, and the 1997 Angler of the Year Award from *Fly Rod and Reel* magazine.

He is in the IFGA Fishing Hall of Fame, the Fresh Water Fishing Hall of Fame, the Fly Fishing Hall of Fame, and the Catskill Fly Fishing Center and Museum Hall of Fame. He also has been an advisor to Trout Unlimited and the Federation of Fly Fishers and has received numerous awards from these organizations. Even with all of these accolades, he still maintains a down-to-earth personality.

If you have picked up a fly rod or tying vise, you have been affected by this humble man. Lefty's saltwater flavorings have added a lot of spice to my flies and fishing. ◆

Gary LaFontaine

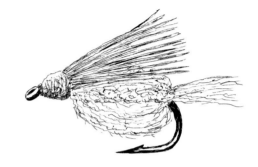

LaFontaine Emergent Caddis Pupa

I CAN REMEMBER THE FIRST TIME I fished a Gary LaFontaine pattern. It was a #16 Black Sparkle Caddis Emerger on the Firehole River, and it was the first spring that I worked for Jack Dennis—I believe the year was 1985. For those familiar with the Jackson area, spring fly fishing can be very limited. April fishing is great on the Snake, but when runoff starts around the first of May, the stream fishing is over for a while. I call this limbo season, because many of the area lakes still have ice on them. Memorial Day weekend brings relief, with the opening day for Yellowstone National Park and Idaho waters. The most common destinations are the Henry's Fork in Idaho or the Firehole in Yellowstone National Park. A two-hour drive from Jackson takes you to these two great early-season fisheries.

The Firehole is fun, not only because of the fishing, but because it is like a trip to another planet—geysers going off around you, watching out for elk on your back cast, and bison blocking your access to a pool. While the Firehole can get high and tea colored, this drainage is much less affected by the whims of snowmelt than other adjacent drainages. One of the consistent early hatches is a small black caddis, and as with many caddis hatches, emerging pupae are a favored trout food. On the day prior to my weekend, I mentioned to Bruce James, the head guide at Jack Dennis, that I was headed to the Firehole. I knew that he had years of experience fishing and guiding on this water, and he told me I had to have some #16 Black LaFontaine Sparkle Caddis Emergers. I wasn't familiar with the fly, so I looked at the flies in the bin and looked up the recipe. The Antron yarn was new to me and I bought a few packages. The next couple of nights, I tied up some of the Sparkle Caddis emergers for my Firehole trip. This was an odd-looking fly, but if it worked, what the hell. I took it to the Firehole, and around mid-morning as the caddis hatch started, I tied one on. Whenever I found a fish consistently rising to caddis, a good drift with the fly seemed to bring out a reaction. The odd-looking fly worked. After fishing it, I was curious why it was effective. This led to a reading session, and I found out that the trilobal nylon Antron fibers captured air bubbles; that trait was common on many emerging caddis larvae. This was also the first time I had intentionally tied a fly with a trailing shuck.

LaFontaine's use of Antron revolutionized the trailing shuck. Other materials were used before this, and Swisher and Richards are the best known for that work. However, when the air-bubble-trapping Antron came into use, it became the standard. The material is readily available, comes in the necessary colors, and is easy to work with. Almost all the other shuck materials in common use today can trace their use back to Gary's initial caddis emerger.

Through Jack Dennis, I was able to spend a little time with Gary. I helped out with a Traveling Fly Fisherman gig in Salt Lake (Jack, Gary, and Mike Lawson—also known to us affectionately as the Three Amigos). I did a few sports shows for Jack Dennis Sports and Snake River Books, and invariably the Three Amigos were there. After hours, dinners and drinks were fun and I got to know Gary and Mike. With this crew, conversation often drifted off to important subjects like fishing and flies. On one occasion, I rowed a film boat as Jack and Gary filmed *Tying and Fishing Attractor Patterns*, and I was able to see Gary in action. I was privileged to spend some time with him.

The most important things I learned from Gary were to have fun and think. At times, he was the ultimate devil's advocate. I can still see his friendly smirk as he tested me. He loved to analyze flies and fishing and find out why they worked. Gary was a great experimenter and would try different materials and theories on trout. His background as a psychologist sometimes made him psychoanalyze his fishing

Grey Emergent Caddis Pupa

and flies, but it was done in an informative and fun way. Time with Gary and reading his works made me think about what material I should use on a fly and why. Having a conversation with Gary always got your brain working. As much as he enjoyed teaching, I think he wanted you to learn how to teach yourself. To me this is a sign of a superior instructor. Even when ALS had robbed his physical abilities, you could see the twinkle of excitement in his eyes when he saw you tying flies and you talked about fishing.

LaFontaine

GREY EMERGENT CADDIS PUPA (tied by Gary LaFontaine)

Hook – Standard dry fly, size 14 – 18
Thread – Black 6/0
Shuck – Grey Antron Sparkle Yarn
Overbody – Grey Antron Sparkle
Underbody – Dubbed grey Sparkle Yarn and fur
Wing – Dark natural deer hair
Head – Grey fur dubbing

Gary's writing career spanned almost forty years, and he had an early start at writing his first magazine article at the age of fifteen. His informative articles have appeared in numerous fishing and fly-fishing magazines. His first book, *Challenge of the Trout,* was published in 1976, and in 1981, his book *Caddisflies* put that prolific insect on the map. It is still the authoritive work on caddisflies. However, it was his later books, *The Dry Fly–New Angles* and *Trout Flies–Proven Patterns,* that had the greatest influence on me. In 1990, after *The Dry Fly–New Angles* came out, an important tying client of mine sent the book along with a large order for the book flies. I probably would have tied and fished some of these anyway, but this was accelerated by the order. Some of my mistakes and intentional ties made their way into my box and onto the river. The Halo Mayfly Emerger in a Pale Morning Dun color quickly became a favorite. The book also made me think about other flies in my box—why they worked and what I could do to improve them. When *Trout Flies–Proven Patterns* arrived three years later, my client had another large order. I was tying and experimenting with Gary's flies again. The concepts for the flies and the fishing logs were most informative, and here again, my brain got a workout. Even when I didn't completely agree with Gary, I could always say he made a good, viable argument. The flies that stuck most in my mind were the Flex-Hopper, the Flex-Stone, and the Flex-Cicada. The concept of a large mobile imitation made sense. I experimented with the idea and then put it in the back of my mind. A decade later, a hopper infestation on Wyoming's Flat Creek pulled the idea out from my mind's archives. To speed up tying, I substituted a rabbit tail for the jointed body and my Mystery Meat Hopper (Rabbit Ass Hopper) was born. I think it works as well as anything for tough terrestrial feeding fish.

Gary has left an important legacy for others to learn from, and even with his shortened life, he has given us all more than a lifetime of knowledge. ◆

MIKE LAWSON

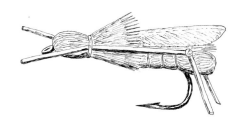

Lawson Henry's Fork Hopper

ONE OF MY EARLY MEMORIES OF MIKE LAWSON is from the video *Tying Western Dry Flies*, which he did with Jack Dennis. In the introduction to the Henry's Fork Hopper, he commented on hopper legs. In the classic, slow Lawson drawl, which might be mistaken for something from the South, he said, "I'm not really a leg man." This was followed by a delayed smirk. Mike's spring-creek patterns, techniques, and ideas were important influences to a young man living in the attractor fly world of Jackson Hole.

As with many other people in this book, I met Mike through Jack Dennis. Initially, I saw his tying instructions and patterns in books, videos, and DVDs produced by Jack. Later, through Jack, I met Mike and Sheralee (Mike's wife) in person. Mike was the first spring-creek expert that I met, and on trips to the Henry's Fork, I would stop at Henry's Fork Anglers and talk to Mike. I learned quite a bit about his home river and its bugs through our conversations. Since that time, I have had the chance to spend some time with Mike at sports shows, parties, and the Traveling Fly Fisherman events.

Lawson's No-Hackle instruction in *Tying Dry Trout Flies* made it possible for me to tie a decent No-Hackle. Prior to this, I made fishable versions, but with these tips, I was finally able to make the wide, balanced wings. His version of Vince Marinaro's Thorax Dun simplified an effective fly and made it attainable to the average tier. Sheralee's Spent Partridge Caddis was the first caddis "spinner" that I had seen, and it was an influence on my low-floating caddis patterns. Before this, I had always used heavily hackled flies. The Henry's Fork Yellow Sally was one of the first specific small stoneflies that I saw and fished. This led to some of my flies, which imitate this important and overlooked hatch. The list of great imitative Lawson patterns is almost endless. The Hemingway Caddis, E-Z Caddis, Partridge Caddis Emerger, and Half Back Emerger are just the tip of the iceberg. While Mike is known as a spring-creek tier, flies like his Black Rubber Legs and Woolhead Sculpin are great flies for big fish in heavy water, and they demonstrate his diversity.

The most direct fly influence from Mike was his Henry's Fork Hopper. This fly was the catalyst for my Foam Wing Hopper and, in turn, my Mystery Meat Hopper. The Henry's Fork Hopper is one the best terrestrials for tough fish. This fly was created when Mike needed a better hopper. The shape was borrowed from the Bennet's Pontoon Hopper popularized by Vince Marinaro. The realistic profile and flush floating design help it mimic the profile of a natural in the water. The aerodynamic bullet head is nice for casting against the bank during the windy days that put this trout fare on the water. I've fished this fly quite a bit on waters like Flat Creek, but I needed to modify it for float fishing. I added a foam wing and legs to the fly to fill a need, and my Foam Wing Hopper was created. This variation on Mike's fly has proven to be effective for me throughout the West, and I get reports from anglers across the country on its productivity.

Mike grew up in Sugar City, Idaho. This eastern Idaho town is located near the Teton River and close to the Lower Henry's River. Although they didn't know it at the time, Mike Lawson and Jack Dennis played baseball against each other in their youth. It is a small world. Outdoor recreation was standard fare in the area, and Mike learned to fish and hunt from his father and grandfather. He started tying when he was fourteen years old with a mail-order set of tools and materials from Herter's. With limited local resources for materials, he rummaged up materials from the local wildlife and livestock. Without a tying book to learn from, he would take apart flies he bought at the town's mercantile. Emory Thomas, the owner of the mercantile, was a fly-fisherman, and Mike would spend time there talking fly fishing with him. With practice, the self-taught tier became proficient.

Henry's Fork Hopper

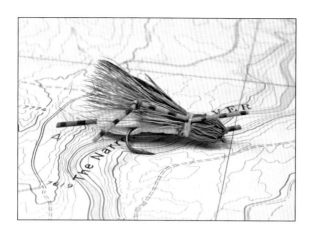

Mike married Sheralee in 1971 and started teaching school that year. He taught industrial arts, drafting, and crafts at South Fremont Junior High for six years. In that eventful year he also met Rene Harrop. Rene had a commercial tying operation, and by 1973, Mike and Sheralee were tying flies for the Harrops to augment Mike's teaching salary. Prior to meeting Mike, Sheralee wasn't a fly-fisherman or tier, but she did come from a fishing and camping family. Mike and Rene became good friends and ended up fishing and tying

Lawson

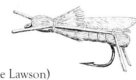

HENRY'S FORK HOPPER (tied by Mike Lawson)

Hook – TMC 5212, sizes 6 – 14
Thread – Yellow 3/0
Body – Cream elk rump
Underwing – Dull yellow dyed elk hair
Wing – Mottled tan/brown hen feather coated with cement
Head – Dark elk
Legs – Knotted tan barred rubber legs

together. Around that time, *Selective Trout* by Swisher and Richards, *Hatches* by Caucci and Natasi, and *Nymphs* by Schwiebert were published. These books greatly influenced the tying and angling of these two and put them on a search of their own for better flies and methods. They took the Swisher and Richards patterns and fine-tuned them, and through commercial tying, the flies made it into the boxes of many anglers.

In 1976, the Lawsons and Harrops started Henry's Fork Anglers in Last Chance. This was a big commitment for the two families with young mouths to feed, and although it would have been great to have the shop together, the economics weren't there. After about a year, the Lawsons took over the shop end of the business and the Harrops continued the tying business. As the shop goes into its thirtieth year in a new location, Henry's Fork Anglers is still the mecca for fishermen seeking flies and information on the Henry's Fork.

Good ideas need to published, and besides the Jack Dennis publications in which Mike has appeared, he has written for most of the best fly-fishing magazines. He also co-authored *Fly Fishing the Henry's Fork* with Gary LaFontaine. The epitome of his works is his book *Spring Creeks*, published in 2003 by Stackpole Books. It is the most comprehensive work on fishing spring creeks and tailwaters and a must-have for the Spring Creek angler. In 1990, Gary LaFontaine prodded Mike to write the book and helped him with an outline. The book took thirteen years to finish, but it held a lifetime of knowledge and was quickly acquired by a mass of excited anglers. Mike is in high demand for seminars around the country. He also is on the pro staff of Sage Rods, Action Optics, Scientific Anglers, and Columbia Sportswear, and he is one of the preeminent contact tiers for Umpqua Feather Merchants.

To protect the waters he loves, Mike is active in conservation and was one of the founding members of the Henry's Fork Foundation. He is also on the board of the Jackson Hole One Fly and is active with Trout Unlimited, the Nature Conservancy, the Federation of Fly-Fishers, and the Teton Regional Land Trust.

The next generation of Lawsons continues the fly-fishing tradition. As with most family businesses, these family members worked at Henry's Fork Anglers in their youth and became accomplished anglers.

Sons Shaun and Chris are flytiers as well; Shaun also manages South Fork Lodge, and Chris guides for Henry's Fork Anglers. Jeanette, although a teacher by profession, spends her recreational time on the water.

In the future, I look forward to spending time with Mike and, of course, learning a thing or two from a spring-creek expert and master tier. ◆

CRAIG MATTHEWS

Matthews' Sparkle Dun

CRAIG MATTHEWS' INFLUENCE ON FLIES and conservation is felt throughout the world. As an innovative tier, his patterns are fished every day on different continents, and his conservation efforts protect trout, bonefish, wildlife, and the surroundings. His Sparkle Duns and X-Caddis have provided me with some great days of fishing and with building blocks for some of my own patterns. Craig's books and articles gave me much-needed information about the insects and patterns for the Greater Yellowstone region. His innovative saltwater flies were also influential and taught me about saltwater flies from a match-the-hatch angle. His conservation efforts and promotion help ensure that future generations will enjoy the resources of the Greater Yellowstone area and places around the world.

Craig's matching combos of his mayfly Sparkle Dun and his caddis-based X-Caddis are simple, well-thought-out flies that work just about anywhere. The Sparkle Dun has been one of my go-to flies for mayfly hatches for years. It's fairly visible and quick to tie, and best of all, fish eat it. I don't know if there is a non-refusal fly, but this is pretty close. My Foam Back Sparkle is based on this pattern except that I added a little thin foam back to allow me to use a larger gap hook.

On a June afternoon many years ago, I was fishing on the Railroad Ranch section of the Henry's Fork. I walked the banks looking for rising fish, and after a bit I noticed a few caddis on the water. On closer inspection, I found out that they were about size sixteen and yellowish tan in color. It seemed like a smart time to sit down and see if anyone wanted to eat them. After a bit, a few noses started to appear—first small fish and then some better rainbows. I tied on a size sixteen, light-colored Elk Hair Caddis, because that was the closest match in my boxes, and slowly waded into position. I picked a fish and cast to it. After many good drifts, it became obvious that he didn't want my fly. Maybe a caddis emerger would work? I dug back into my boxes, but I didn't have any caddis emergers that color; however, I noticed some size sixteen, sulphur Sparkle Duns. I bent back the wing and changed it into a caddis. I caught some of the smaller fish and managed to fool a couple in the sixteen-inch range. The modification of a good fly saved my butt. This experience, along with my use of Harrop's Hair Wing as both a Pale Morning Dun and Yellow Sally (depending on how I adjusted the wing streamside), led to my Everything Emerger later on that trip.

Around this time, along with John Juracek, Craig authored *Fly Patterns of Yellowstone*. This book was a significant reference for me on natural and artificial flies for Yellowstone and Montana. The book contained many simple, effective patterns from the employees, guides, and customers of Blue Ribbon Flies. It showed how to tie and fish many of the flies and certainly how to fish these and my similar patterns under different conditions. The follow-up publication, *Fishing Yellowstone Hatches,* is the authoritative work on aquatic insects and imitations for the region. The standard hatches are discussed well, but the most important to me is the coverage of localized hatches that are extremely important in specific drainages.

I started tying saltwater flies in the late 1980s, and most of these early flies were attractor-style baitfish and crustaceans. An article that Craig wrote in the early 1990s for *Fly Fisherman* on Turneefe flies opened my eyes to what bonefish eat; I also learned about flies that will imitate the food source. I had dabbled in imitative saltwater flies, but this really made me think. Craig's corresponding flies, like Pop's Bonefish Bitters and Turneefe Crab, are similar to his great trout flies in construction—simple, but with a realistic shape and action. Looking at his patterns has helped me fine-tune my saltwater flies to make them more effective.

Tan X-Caddis, PMD Sparkle Dun

Craig grew up in Grand Rapids, Michigan, and learned to fly fish in the Pentwater, Rogue, and Pere Marquette rivers of lower Michigan. He taught himself to tie flies; Charles Brooks, Joe Brooks, Bud Lilly, Vince Marinaro, and Colonel Harding were big influences on his flies and fishing. Craig graduated from Michigan State University as the valedictorian of the police academy and started his first career in law enforcement. He met his wife, Jackie, while he was working as a cop; she was a dispatcher in Michigan. For many years, he made an annual trip to the Yellowstone River and Yellowstone National Park in September or October to hit the fall fishing.

In 1979, with the attraction of the water and Jackie's encouragement, he moved from Grand Rapids, Michigan, to West Yellowstone to become the police chief. It was general knowledge that most police chiefs didn't last very long in "West," and he was encouraged by Nick Lyons and Bud and Greg Lilly to start a fly-tying operation as a backup. Jackie started the company, Blue Ribbon Flies, and employed handicapped tiers, while Craig took care of the law. The operation was named after the "Blue Ribbon" streams that inundate the area. Craig spent three years as the police chief before making fly fishing a full career. Since then, Blue Ribbon Flies has become one of the best-known fly shops in the region and the Mecca for prime fly-tying materials.

One of Craig's favorite waters in the Greater Yellowstone is the Madison River. It has influenced his fly designs and conservation efforts. To quote Craig, "I guess what attracts me to the Madison is its lovely valley, the diversity of the river as to its fish, hatches, water types. I fish the river for a hundred days yearly, usually not full days but a lot of evenings and afternoons, and I'm always amazed at its uniqueness and beauty!"

Craig's trout flies are standards in most fly boxes. The Sparkle Dun and the corresponding X-Caddis are very effective patterns during mayfly and caddis hatches, and added bonuses are the simplicity of construction and their visibility. Other patterns, such as the Iris Caddis, the Matthews Cranefly, the Z-lon Midge, the Knock Down Dun, the Bead Head Serendipity, and the Foam Wing Spinner, have a following with trout and the angler.

West Yellowstone winters are very long, and the chance to fish in the tropics is very tempting. Craig and Jackie spend a lot of time fishing in Belize and the Bahamas. Craig's knack for understanding flies isn't lost in the salt. He was one of the first to actively try to imitate bonefish food. The patterns he devised for the picky Turneefe Island bonefish are now being used around the world and include Pop's Bonefish Bitters, Sir Mantis, Salsa Shrimp, and Clam Before the Storm. He is a contract tier for Umpqua Feather Merchants, which makes his flies readily available to anglers around the world.

Craig has written some of the best books on area flies, hatches, and waters. *Fly Patterns of Yellowstone, Volume 1,* and *Fishing Yellowstone Hatches* were co-authored along with former Blue Ribbon partner John Juracek and are must-reads for those fishing in the area. Recently, they did a companion DVD to *Fishing Yellowstone Hatches;* Craig also did a DVD on *Fly Tying Yellowstone Hatches.* In addition, he co-authored *The Yellowstone Fly-Fishing Guide* along with Clayton Mollinero. *Western Fly-Fishing Strategies,* by Craig, teaches the methods for fishing the area's waters. His writings can be found on the pages of many fly-fishing magazines and in a variety of books.

Craig is active in protecting the environment, and he commits time and money to it. Since 1997, Blue Ribbon Flies has committed 2 percent of its sales to environmental causes. In 2001, along with Patagonia's Yvon Chouinard, Craig started the One Percent for the Planet Club. Members pledge 1 percent of their gross sales to environmental causes. Craig is also a Founder of the Yellowstone Park Foundation, which is active in protecting and reestablishing native species such as the West Slope Cutthroat. He is the stewardship director for Montana Trout Unlimited and was instrumental in helping fund projects for the Montana Trout Foundation, the River Network—Conservancy, the Yellowstone Association, the Federation of Fly Fishers, the Henry's Fork Foundation, and the Henry's Lake Foundation.

In the past, he has been on the board of the Nature Conservancy of Montana, the Montana Trout Foundation, and the West Yellowstone Cooperative Fisheries Foundation. He arranged the West Slope

Matthews

(tied by Craig Matthews)

TAN X-CADDIS

Hook – TMC 100 standard dry fly, sizes 14 – 18
Thread – 8/0 olive
Shuck – Amber Zelon
Body – Tan Blue Ribbon sparkle Dubbing
Wing – Mottled natural deer
Head – Butts of wing

PMD SPARKLE DUN

Hook – TMC 100 standard dry fly, sizes 16 – 20
Thread – Light Olive 8/0
Shuck – Amber Zelon
Body – Fine PMD dubbing
Wing – Sparkle Dun deer hair

Cutthroat Cooperative Meeting. In 1993, Craig and Blue Ribbon Flies were awarded the Nature Conservancy's business award for preserving wild trout habitat. In 1997, Yellowstone National Park Superintendent Michael Finley recognized them as a Protector of Yellowstone, and in 2002, they received a plaque from Montana Fish, Wildlife, and Parks honoring them for their help in acquiring the Three Dollar Bridge site on the Madison.

When they aren't fishing, tying, or getting involved in conservation, Craig and Jackie Matthews travel, teaching fly-tying classes and fly-fishing strategy classes and giving presentations on their favorite trout and bonefish waters. ◆

Franz B. Pott

Pott Sandy Mite

IF YOU LOOK AT THE HISTORY OF WESTERN FLY TYING, it is impossible to ignore the hair hackle Pott flies of a bygone era. How can you tell where you are going if you don't know where you came from? In the not-too-distant past, they formed the backbone of fly selections. The man, Franz B. Pott, left us long ago, but his influence on Greater Yellowstone flies and fishing is huge. His Sandy Mite was comparable to the Parachute Adams of today; everyone had some in their boxes, and they were effectively fished in all kinds of water. The Pott flies are almost a chicken-or-the-egg argument. Was western fly fishing created by the flies, or were the flies created by the fishing? At a minimum, they were responsible for a few generations of western anglers becoming fly-fishermen, which in turn paved the way for my tying and fishing. Maybe some other flies would have filled the big void, but that is a big "what if." Even today, they are good caddis larvae and pupae imitations.

The Pott flies were some of the first patterns that I can remember seeing in local fly bins, and they were clearly visible in the aluminum-clip Perrine fly boxes used by my dad and friends' fathers. Along with Gray Hackle Yellows and Brown Hackle Peacocks, the wet flies ruled the roost. In my youth, there were plenty of anglers who fished only these patterns, and they caught plenty of fish. When I was growing up, the Pott flies could be found in about any fly shop or sporting goods store and even in rural gas and pop stands.

I can remember an early experience with a Pott fly when I was about thirteen. I was at Tracy Wigwam Boy Scout Camp in Mill Creek Canyon near Salt Lake City. This was the standard scout camp and we did a number of different outdoor activities. Of course, one of the activities was fishing on Mill Creek. Among our group, a handful of fish was caught during the week, and we figured there weren't very many trout in the stream. Around the end of the week, we found out differently. We were weaving lace keychains at a station near the stream, and I noticed an older gentleman in big canvas waders wading downstream and swinging a fly through pockets. He was picking up trout in places where our offerings went ignored. My craft project ceased as I watched this master vacuum the stream. I was impressed. I went over and did the usual, "What are the fish eating?" He held up a light-colored Pott fly, probably a Lady Mite. I remembered the fly and went home and tried to tie some. At the time, I didn't know the correct way to tie the Pott flies, but I made up wet flies that looked kind of like them. Fortunately, my surrogate Pott flies caught a few fish.

I've fished Pott-style flies with success over the years. Mine use a bullet-head-style hair hackle rather than the official woven technique. Dan Bailey and others used this modification as well. For the 2001 Whitefish Can't Jump Contest in Livingston, Montana, I used a hair hackle fly to win the event. This was a spin-off of the Jackson Hole One Fly Contest and was an April fund-raiser for the Federation of Fly Fishers Museum. You can only use a single fly for the one-day event. Whitefish are plus points, and those evil trout are minus points. All spring, during *Baetis* time, I was catching a bunch of rainbows on a #16 Soft Hackle Bead Head Pheasant Tail Nymph. I was also hooking a bunch of whitefish. I knew this was the fly pattern to use for the contest, but I needed to modify it for strength. A dubbed pheasant tail colored body with heavy wire rib made sense, and I used squirrel tail hair in place of the hen hackle. It looked like the original, but it was more durable. I caught seventy whitefish and seven trout in about five hours, and the fly looked as good at the end as it did in the beginning. The old hair hackle–style fly had worked again.

Sandy Mite

Other anglers asked me how I caught that many fish, and I told them, "You know those days when the whitefish won't leave you alone and you move on? I didn't."

The reason for hair hackle flies throws off many contemporary anglers, where we have been conditioned to using only soft mobile materials on sub-surface imitations. Hair hackle wet flies are basically soft hackles for heavy water. They are frequently swung down and across like a wet fly or soft hackle,

Pott

SANDY MITE (tied by Pott Fly Company)

Hook – Mustad 9485 wet fly, size 6 – 12
Thread – Black 3/0
Body – Sandy colored ox hair
Belly stripe – Orange thread
Hackle – Woven sand ox hair

but the stiffer hair hackle stays away from the body of the fly and won't fold down against the body like softer materials. The stiffer hair will actually have more action in the strong current than hen hackle and will pulsate rather than collapse. Hair hackles are also very durable and give a big profile reminiscent of large caddis pupae or stonefly nymphs. An interesting parallel to the woven Montana flies is the stiff-hackled Coq de Leon wet flies of Spain's Pyrenees and the woven bodies of the World Champion Polish and Czech Nymphs. The European patterns look very similar to the Pott flies, and both fly types evolved for separate but similar conditions—fast currents, with lots of caddis flies and stoneflies. On closer examination, the segmented body of the Pott fly is very similar to a net-spinning or free-living caddis larva.

Details of Franz Pott's life are vague. I picked up most of the details from reading George Grant's works and talking with Mike Wilkerson, who was the last proprietor of the Pott Fly Company. Rumor has it that Pott was a German wig maker who immigrated to the United States in the late teens or early twenties. The fact part is that he had a barbershop in Missoula, Montana, and also made wigs on the side. In the early 1920s, fly tying also became a pastime and occupation, and Pott's history of hair weaving made woven flies a logical step. There is some controversy over who made the first woven western patterns, but Pott was the largest producer, had his own patterns, and certainly put them on the map. He also had a 1925 patent on a woven body, and in 1934 he patented the Pott fly body and hackle. The commercial production of Pott's hair hackle flies started in the 1920s, and he employed local women to make the flies. Pott marketed his flies throughout the region. He had a reputation for being very critical of how the flies were tied and had a cantankerous side. He was also demanding of his dealers and sometimes would tell them what they had to buy.

Most of the flies are made with ox or badger hair with a heavy-thread belly weave. The distinct pattern of the colored thread on the belly of the fly identifies it as a Pott fly. Wet flies were common at the time for a couple of reasons: They worked, and fishing dry flies on heavy currents was difficult to do with the tackle of the day. They didn't have high-floating plastic fly lines, nylon tippets, or strong, light-wire hooks at that time.

Franz Pott passed away in the mid 1950s, and the Pott Fly Company has been through five owners since Pott. From the 1920s to the 1960s, the Pott flies were some of the most popular flies in Montana and throughout the West, and they still have a following today. Unfortunately, Mike Wilkerson had to terminate the Pott Fly Company a few years ago due to the lack of hackle weavers. Because of age and attrition, he was losing the tiers of these classic flies. If you find some, do yourself a favor and buy a piece of fly history.

Next time you look at a modern segmented caddis larva, or woven-body nymph, realize that you might be staring at a direct descendant of a Missoula wig maker, and know that at a minimum, the fly is an important part of western fly-fishing tradition. ◆

Bob Quigley

Quigley Cripple

Bob Quigley's Cripple is a wonderful fly for tough fish and is synonymous with the suspended emerger. If you want to describe a partially sunken emerger, mention a Quigley and everyone knows what you are talking about. In many ways, it's kind of like Kleenex is to facial tissue. Through the Quigley Cripple, I learned the importance of this important insect stage, and it has led to the creation of some of my own suspended patterns.

I first saw the fly years ago when I was putting out a big spring fly pre-season order at the Jack Dennis Outdoor Shop. This was a huge project and involved sorting the flies, organizing them, and putting them into the bins. While this was work, it was also fun. You had the chance to see all of the new patterns. I noticed an interesting fly labeled the Quigley Cripple. It had a dark-colored marabou tail and matching body, with a light-colored thorax. It also had a wing that went over the hook eye and a hackle over the base of the wing. It didn't look like anything I had seen before. I asked about the fly and found out that it was tied to imitate a mayfly in the transition from nymph to adult. I tied some of the flies and tried them. I was pleasantly surprised with the results. In particular, they worked well on the Henry's Fork and on the flat-water sections of the Firehole. When Flat Creek opened, the Quigley Cripples also proved their worth. My Parachute Midge Emerger and PFD Emerger evolved from using the Quigley Cripple.

The cripple, or stuck-in-the-shuck concept, is important in fooling selective trout. The transition of a mayfly from nymph to dun makes it very vulnerable. It is part nymph and part dun, but without the escape mechanisms of either, and the efficient predatory instincts of selective trout lead them to easy food sources. They aren't smart—they are looking for an easy meal. An insect stuck at the surface is one of these.

Bob grew up in San Jose, California, and his father started him fishing with a fly rod at the age of six. Frequently, there would be a live hopper on the end, and this led to Bob's addiction to surface fishing. By the time he was nine, he was tying his own flies. Without the luxury of a local fly shop, he scrounged up what materials he could and learned his methods from library books. As he developed his talents, he started tying flies for family members and friends, and by the time he was fourteen, fly tying was his livelihood. This was the start of a lifetime career. He fished the local steelhead and trout streams, bass ponds, Sierras, and San Francisco Bay for stripers. With relatives in Oregon and in Ketchum, Idaho, he expanded his fishing repertoire. On many of these trips he took the bus to visit them and tied flies on the way. The irresponsibility of youth allowed him to fish many waters in the days of almost no fishing pressure, and have hundred-fish days on dry flies.

An important influence on his tying and fishing was Del Brown, the permit guru. Bob inadvertently met Del when Bob trespassed across Del's property on the way to go steelhead fishing. Del took a liking to him and influenced Bob's tying by encouraging him to experiment with his fly patterns. Bob tied trout and steelhead flies for him, and together they came up with new angles and experimental flies.

Many of Bob's original patterns are based on fishing problems, where the fishing wasn't as easy as it should be. With all the time Bob spends on the water, he has plenty of opportunities to observe trout and try out new patterns. His best-known fly, the Quigley Cripple, came about this way. In the mid 1970s, Bob opened a small fly shop in a lodge on California's Fall River and guided the lodge's clients. This water was known for prolific hatches and selective large trout. His own time on the water and time with clients gave him a fast-forward on the learning curve.

Mahogany Dun Cripple, Olive PMD Marabou Cripple, PMD Pheasant Tail Cripple

During a PMD hatch in the summer of 1978, Bob was fishing a Hair Spider. This pattern, which was a sparsely tied Horner Deer Hair adaptation similar to a Humpy, was popular with old-timers on the Fall River. A number of these variations were tied with or without hackle. On this day, the fish were rising around Bob's fly, eating the natural and leaving his artificial alone. He did manage to catch some fish, and, through doing so, the fly became ragged and waterlogged. The back of the fly was sinking while the front hung in the

Quigley Cripples

(tied by Bob Quigley)

MAHOGANY DUN CRIPPLE

Hook – Standard dry fly, sizes 14 – 16
Thread – Black 6/0
Shuck – Brown Z-Lon barred with black marker
Body – Brown marabou
Rib – Black 3/0 thread
Wing – Natural deer
Hackle – Dark dun

OLIVE PMD MARABOU CRIPPLE

Hook – Emerger hook, sizes 14 – 18
Thread – Yellow 6/0
Shuck – Tan Z-Lon and yellow Krystal Flash
Abdomen – Light olive marabou
Rib – Brown thread
Thorax – Pale yellow dubbing
Wing – Natural deer
Hackle – Light dun

PMD PHEASANT TAIL CRIPPLE

Hook – Emerger hook, sizes 14 – 18
Thread – Yellow 6/0
Shuck – Brown Z-Lon
Abdomen – Pheasant tail fibers
Rib – Fine copper wire
Thorax – Pale yellow dubbing
Wing – Natural deer
Hackle – Natural golden ginger

film. All of a sudden, the fly really started to work, and the fish were moving to eat it. When he wore out the first fly, Bob roughed up the other Hair Spiders in his box prior to fishing them, and the half-below-the-water, half-above-the-water concept worked on the new flies.

When the hatch ended, it was time to work out a better fly. Bob went to work at the vise. The rear body of the fly was tied in the color of a PMD shuck and nymph, and as you moved up the hook shank, the fly transcended into the thorax color of an adult PMD, just like a dun struggling out of a nymphal shuck. A reverse-tied wing of deer hair was used as an emerging wing and indicator and maintained the shape of the original Hair Spider. The butts of the wing had the added benefit of looking like a split-wing case. The hackle held up the head of the fly and imitated the legs of the natural in the surface film, while the body suspended down below the surface. The new pattern proved to be very effective, and in a short time, with the help of shop tiers and guides, Quigley came up with a series of cripples to match the major mayfly hatches. Not only had Bob solved a PMD problem, the Quigley Cripple turned into a viable pattern for almost all of the mayfly hatches that occur in the world. From Brown Drakes to Tricos, it is a "go to" pattern. It can also be used with success during midge and caddis hatches.

The basic concept of the Quigley Cripple can be tied in different sizes and colors and with various materials. Bob is constantly tinkering with the fly to match a certain need. Standard dry-fly hooks are used on most of the flies, but larger-gap, curved-shank hooks sink the abdomen more quickly and have a natural-looking profile; they also offer greater strength. These are referred to as Humpbacks. Marabou was the original shuck and pulsates in the water; however, Antron and Z-lon are more durable and have a shuck-like sheen to them. Most of Bob's Cripples are tied with deer or elk hair due their durability, but in some situations, he uses CDC. Flash is also sometimes added to the wing to imitate the shimmer of a moving mayfly wing. The amount of hackle used can be changed to match water velocity. Less hackle is better in flat water, and a heavier hackle gives more flotation in choppy water. Besides using the normal chicken hackle, Bob also uses emu hackles on some of his flies—another Quigley innovation. This gives a slightly rough, buggy look. In some cases, he even uses rubber legs. The versatility and adaptability of the simple design add to its appeal.

Bob's fly creations go way beyond the Cripple. His Loop Wing Parachutes and Loopy Stackers are great spring-creek patterns. Bud Chatam used one of Bob's Loop Wing Parachutes during the 2004 Jackson Hole. He landed fifty-three fish and easily outscored other anglers who were fishing that section of river—proof that the fly works and is well tied. Bob's Hackle Stacker series of flies covers everything from small spring mayflies to large golden stones and hoppers. For these flies, Bob wraps the hackle around a mono strand and pulls it over the thorax. This gives the trout the smooth belly of the natural with the hackle over it in a realistic leg profile. The Stacker Duns use this style of hackle to make a Comapradun-style wing that has favor with many sophisticated anglers.

Quigley's patterns have been produced by a number of major fly companies, including Umpqua, Frontier Flies, and now Idylwilde Flies. At one time, Bob was a sales rep for Frontier Flies. Bob has written for many of the fly-fishing magazines and in doing so has shared his patterns and insights with the rest of us. In 2004, a DVD of his flies, *Tying Bob Quigley's Signature Flies* was produced.

Great flies keep emerging from Bob's vise, and their influence on tying and fishing gets the notice of trout and anglers. ◆

Rainy Riding

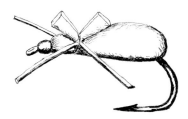

Rainy Foam Beetle

Rainy Riding is the First Lady of Foam and an important innovator in the use of synthetic materials. Through her flies, materials, and marketing, she has brought foam flies into the mainstream. Foam had been the domain of the warm-water world, but Rainy helped to put foam flies on the trout map. Early foam trout flies were pretty rudimentary, and while they caught fish, most conservative trout fishermen wouldn't be caught with one on the end of their line. Rainy's approach was to incorporate foam into accepted patterns that had traditional hair and hackle components. This made them more appealing to the traditional angler than full-on-foam flies.

A good part of Rainy's influence came from her materials. Her Float Foam was the first common round foam on the market and made it easy to make aesthetic-looking foam bodies. She was a marketing genius and included great illustrated tying instructions for her patterns with her Float Foam. How could you not tie them? Her foam flies and materials have expanded over the years, and the spectrum goes from small, match-the-hatch patterns to large offshore creations. To quote her son Jesse, "I showed her a new product idea I found just the other day, and when I checked on her again, there she was, using it for something I would have never thought of on a fly. Her mind just never stops thinking, dreaming of new fly ideas." Rainy is an integral part of flies moving into this century.

I learned of Rainy through her flies, videos, and materials, and I met her in person for the first time in April 1994 at the first East Idaho Fly Tying Expo in Idaho Falls. Watching her tie, I knew what I liked about her—her tying was fluid, well done, and simple. When I got back to Jackson, we called in an order for her foam and for some other materials. Her small foam ants and beetles were a revelation to me and convinced me to fish these overlooked flies. I can remember many days on spring creeks and slow-water side channels where my variation on her ants and beetles saved the day. They were simple and floated better than the hair or dubbing versions. These are my "go to" spring-creek flies. She is also one of the first well-known tiers to incorporate cyanoacrylate "super glue" into their tying. Like I need an excuse to use more adhesive, but this accelerated my use of super glue. Over the years, I've sold materials to Rainy, bought materials from her, and learned from her. Every year, I look forward to seeing her at the Fly Fishing Retailer Show for a nice chat, a warm smile, and a big hug.

Rainy was born in rural Roosevelt, Utah, and lived there most of her life. At age five, her grandfather started her on her lifelong passion of fly fishing. She enjoyed the outdoors, and as Rainy recalls, "I was definitely a tomboy until my high school years." She waited to tie flies until she was twenty-one, when Art Jones, a professor at the Utah State University Extension in Roosevelt, taught her to tie and became her mentor. Jack Dennis's tying books were also a huge influence, and they helped her refine some of her standard techniques. They were, as she remembers, "the first good how-to books on the market." She always dreamed of meeting Jack and eventually she did. A book by George Grant inspired her to develop her talent to become as good and creative as he was. Beyond the books and initial tying instruction, she is a self-taught tier and has developed her own patterns and time-saving techniques. Her tying motto is, "It takes just as much time to tie a bad fly as it does a good one. . . . Might as well be a perfect one."

Rainy always had a room in her house where she tied and offered a few hooks, thread, dubbing, and flies, but she got hard-core into the commercial tying business in 1974, when she put an ad in *Fly Fishing the West* and *Field and Stream.* This substantially increased her business to fifteen accounts, and one of these

Rainy's Foam Beetle

fly accounts was Raymond Rumpf, the large East Coast tackle distributor. She was now deeply entrenched in commercial tying.

Foam has been integral to her flies and business, and through its use she has developed her own product. The first foam she developed was her Float Foam, which is now a fly-tying standard and the first popular cylindrical foam for trout flies. She felt that if foam could improve flotation and add durability, it would make her flies more marketable. She had Float Foam formulated to make traditional flies ride higher but still keep the same diameter and

Rainy

RAINY'S PROTOTYPE FOAM BEETLES (tied by Rainy Riding)

Hook – Standard dry fly, sizes 8 – 16
Thread – Black 3/0
Body – Black Rainy's Float Foam split in half
Head – The tip of body foam
Legs – Black rubber or black cord
Indicator (optional) – Bright colored foam

color of the original patterns. The development of Rainy's Float Foam started at the end of 1988 and was introduced at the Denver Fly Tackle Dealer Show in 1989. Over the years, Float Foam itself has been reformulated several times to make it last longer and float higher. The illustrated instructions in her Float Foam packaging taught people how to use it, which in turn helped lead to its popularity. The introduction of a material line that could be sold to the public and distributed to fly shops increased her business and made it easier for her to support herself and four children.

Shortly afterwards, more foam products and materials were added to the line. These were developed for personal and trade purposes. Being an avid fly-fisherwoman, she was trying to make her own flies more effective and more visible, and this led to products that would help other anglers and also turn a profit. Rainy has always been a creator of new things and never sits still, especially when it comes to fly tying. This has led to different colors, densities, and types of foam, including parachute posts, damsel and dragonfly bodies, Hi-Vis Ant Bodies, bee bodies, specialty sheet foam, poppers, and unique tools.

Besides the instructions in her foam packages, Rainy has some excellent videos on her flies and tying techniques. These include *Tying Flies with Rainy's Float Foam, Rainy's Favorite Foam Flies, Rainy's Extra Terrestrials 101 and 102*, and *Rainy's Blue Ribbon Flies.* These are great instruction for those who want to learn her methods and expand their use of foam and synthetics.

In 1994, after years of dabbling in fly-fishing retail, Rainy tore down her garage and built a full-service fly shop next to her home in downtown Logan, Utah. The shop was open from 1994 through 1999 and also served as the base for her wholesale business.

In about 1991, she started hiring out locals, usually college students, to help with the growing demand for her flies. This was both good and bad. She increased her capacity, but when the students graduated, she lost a tier whom she had spent years training. The writing was on the wall, and Rainy started investigating the international market for an offshore tying operation. In 1999, she started a small ten-girl operation in Thailand. Within a few months, she was offered a job, along with her business partner and friend, Ellen Clark, to manage the McKenzie fly-tying factory. This factory produced her patterns as well as McKenzie's flies. Within a short time, the Streamworks conglomeration bought out McKenzie, and in a few years, Streamworks was purchased by the Scientific Anglers Division of 3M. Rainy and Ellen now own the factory and have been able to expand their own commercial offerings. With 100 employees, they now have the capacity to supply the demand for Rainy's flies and materials.

Rainy Riding's fertile mind keeps coming up with new and innovative flies, and she is at the leading edge of fly tying. I wonder what new flies she will have at the trade show next year? ◆

SHANE STALCUP

Stalcup CDC Parachute Dun

SHANE STALCUP IS ONE OF THE BRIGHTEST MINDS in modern fly tying. He is best known for his immaculate spring-creek flies, but his fishing and tying go way beyond that. His warm-water and streamer patterns are just as good as his diminutive patterns, and his knowledge of materials is astounding. In the world of similar flies, he has some great original designs that blend the best of natural and synthetic materials. Along with the Harrops, he is the guru of CDC.

While working at the Jack Dennis Outdoor Shop in the 1980s and early 1990s, I saw some of Shane's Umpqua-produced patterns, but when I moved to Austin, Texas, and worked at the Austin Angler, I took full notice. There were a couple of the Umpqua Plexiglas countertop displays in the shop, and an entire slot had mostly Stalcup flies. The flies looked great. They were simple, beautiful ties that screamed "fish will eat me." Later on, when I moved to Livingston, Montana, and started writing, I had the chance to talk to Shane. I was doing a new materials review for *Fly Fisherman Magazine*. I had noticed a few unique-looking materials at the Fly Fishing Retailer Show that were connected to Shane. I called him to get samples, and we had some nice tier-to-tier conversations. When the package arrived, I was more impressed.

Other new products were good, but his jumped out. I had a great time incorporating his materials into flies for instructional photos and descriptions on what to do with materials.

One of the Stalcup flies that impresses me the most is his CDC Parachute Dun. A duck's ass isn't bred the same as genetic hackle, and you need to modify it for many wrapped hackle purposes. You can put CDC fibers in a dubbing loop, but I'm not very fond of dubbing loops. To make a CDC parachute hackle, he ties in a bundle of CDC fibers with a poly yarn clump that will become the wing. He then just pulls up the poly and wraps around the CDC to make it radiate into a hackle. The idea and execution are so simple, they blow you away. It's one of those "why didn't I think of that" moments. In fly tying, the simplest things can be the best. I like the way Shane uses his Medallion Sheeting to make different-style wings in his patterns, ranging from minute emergers to hoppers. Shane uses modern tying adhesives in some creative fashions, like a hot glue snail, a tubing and epoxy scud, and using Softex to bind a marabou tail into a damsel nymph body. Shane is a master at combining natural and synthetic materials to make a better fly. I always look forward to seeing Shane's magazine articles and new flies, and it seems like I learn something every time.

Shane grew up in Fort Collins, Colorado, and started fishing the area's waters with his father at an early age. Like most of us, he evolved from worms to spinners and eventually to flies. In 1981, while on a fishing trip, his father's friend Ed McAvoy showed him how to tie a fly. A spark was ignited, and shortly afterward he had a rudimentary fly-tying kit. As with many basic kits, a manual was lacking, so he experimented and figured things out on his own. Pretty soon his flies looked as good as the commercial ones.

Shane met A.K. Best, a superb commercial tier and fellow Coloradan. This was a fortuitous meeting, and A.K. took him under his wing and became a teacher and good friend. Shane was learning from one of the best, and A.K. convinced him to become a commercial tier. He started getting orders from local shops and had a full-time job tying trout, steelhead, and warm-water flies. This gave Shane a well-rounded education on fly tying that has crossed over into his own designs and materials.

Shane was getting noticed, and while he was at a Federation of Fly Fishers Conclave in the 1980s, Ken Menard of Umpqua Feather Merchants gave him CDC and told him to play with it. A short time later,

Olive CDC Parachute Dun

Bill Black of Umpqua asked Shane to be a contract tier. Some of his new CDC flies made it into the Umpqua catalog, which led to more experimentation at the vise and on the water to make more effective CDC flies. Because of his skills, Shane was commissioned to teach CDC techniques at Umpqua's Thailand factory. Later on, he would also teach fly tying for Solitude flies in their Chinese facility. By the mid 1990s, Shane was well known in fly-fishing and fly-tying circles. Shane's fly patterns are always in demand, and over the years he has also been a contract tier for McKenzie, Targus, and Solitude.

Stalcup

OLIVE CDC PARACHUTE DUN (tied by Scott Sanchez)

Hook – Straight eye, light wire dry fly, sizes 12 – 22
Thread – Olive
Tail – Dark dun mayfly tail
Body – Premium olive dun goose biot
Post – Poly yarn
Hackle – Natural dun CDC
Thorax – Callibaetis fine dry fly dubbing

Even with all of this going on, Shane graduated from the University of North Carolina with a degree in architecture. He could get a job in the East but preferred fishing back home in the West. He figured that since fly tying paid his way through college, he might as well stick to his first career and live where he wanted to be. Maybe he would have been the next Frank Lloyd Wright, but instead, the fly-fishing world kept an artist.

Along with tying, Shane is a materials guru and is constantly experimenting with new stuff and different ways to use it. He has been in the materials business for more than ten years and got into it because he needed better materials to tie his flies. This has led to his own retail business and to sourcing for materials houses. His name on the package sells the goods and for good reason—he has some really cool, innovative stuff. For example, Shane sells premium-grade stretchy plastic tubing and half-round D-Rib. While this stuff is a notch above most vinyl tubing, this is only a small part of the picture. His creative mind has produced some great fly components from his tubing. He crimps the tubing to give it segmentation and then inserts tails into it. His damsel nymph bodies look like they will crawl out of the bag, and the similar Fish Claws are perfect for crawfish, mantis, or snapping shrimp patterns. His hopper legs add a knotted joint and are one of the few super-realistic hopper legs that won't twist your leader. He even uses this material to make segmented trailing shucks.

Shane has been featured in a number of tying videos. Because of his unique flies and reputation, many publications have been after him to write articles and a book. However, Shane was hesitant because he wanted to wait until he became a good photographer, which would give him complete control over the tying sequences. The wait has been worthwhile, and his articles are superb. He has been published in most of the major U.S. magazines and has written for *Tightloop,* a Japanese magazine. His first book, *Mayflies: Top To Bottom,* is an incredible resource of his tested patterns and unique ideas that can be added to your own flies. When I unpacked the box of books at the shop, one of the copies immediately went home to my library. His *Caddisflies: Top To Bottom* will be out shortly, and I'm sure I'll pick one up as soon as it is ready. Through his Japanese connection, he met the Japanese macro-photography expert Toshi Karita, who gave a few tips and supplied photos for Shane's books.

Unknown health problems have made it difficult for Shane to sit for long periods of time, and this has curtailed his commercial tying. However, even with a number of neck and brain surgeries, he keeps an optimistic outlook and has modified his career. He now concentrates on selling his materials and has become a sales representative for some premier fly-fishing and fly-tying products. I wish him the best of luck and hope he will be able to get back at the vise.

When his *Caddisflies: Top To Bottom* book hits the shelves, I wonder what new trick I'll pick up? ◆

DOUG SWISHER

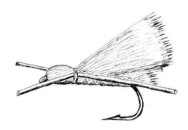

Swisher Madam X

THE WORLD OF TECHNICAL FLY FISHING owes a lot to Doug Swisher and his angling and writing partner, Carl Richards. Their book, *Selective Trout*, was the first major entomology-based book to be published since Vince Marinaro's books in the late 1950s. Doug and Carl brought to light many of the ideas and patterns we take for granted today, especially the importance of cripples. While Doug Swisher is best known for his work on solving imitation, his attractor patterns are equally significant, and his Madam X is a fly that revolutionized western attractor patterns.

I learned to tie flies and fly-fish when I was twelve, and I got into it in a big way. I didn't have anyone to teach me the intricacies, so I voraciously read any fly-tying or fly-fishing book that I could get my hands on. I don't think there was a fly-fishing or fly-tying book at the local library that I didn't check out. One of those books was *Selective Trout* by Doug Swisher and Carl Richards. From it, I learned about match-the-hatch fishing and imitative patterns. When I was growing up in Utah, fly fishing was almost entirely done with attractor patterns, so this was an important revelation for me. I tied a bunch of the flies from the book and fished them. I still have a No Hackle from that time that I tied with plastic wings.

The Madam X was a big influence on me and on western tying in general. I first saw some of these in the mid 1980s, when Jack Dennis came back from Utah's Green River with some flies that Emmett Heath had been using. He gave me the samples and asked me to tie some for clients who were going fishing there. I tied some in different colors for the customers and made a few extras for myself. They looked buggy, and they were simple and cheap to tie.

The first time that I fished the fly was on the Snake River in Grand Teton National Park, on the Deadman's Bar-to-Moose section. I was with my good friend, John Hanlon, and we were having pretty good luck floating and fishing hoppers, Double Humpies, and Wulffs. When we stopped to get out and fish a series of braids, I thought I should give the new fly a spin. I tied on a size eight Madam X with brown rubber legs. John went to one channel and I went to another. In the small side channel was a deep trough adjacent to a log. This was definitely a fishy-looking spot. I made a couple of casts on the near side of the trough just in case a fish might be in there, and then I placed a cast next to the log. A fifteen-inch cutthroat just about did a back flip to get the fly. I brought him in and released him. Then I moved up and caught a few smaller fish in the channel, all of which aggressively ate the fly. On that day, the fish had eaten our normal flies but not with that much gusto. I liked how the new fly worked. At the boat, I gave John some of the Madam Xs, and for the rest of the day, the Lady ruled the roost.

For years, a Madam X with dull orange legs was my fly of choice in Jackson Hole, and I still fish it and variations of it today. It crosses over as a hopper, a golden stone, a brown stone, a crane fly, and, in small sizes, an October caddis. The fly also doubles as a searching fly and a strike indicator. One thing I really like about this pattern is that it can be fished in a variety of ways. When dead drifting them, the rubber has a subtle motion, especially in riffled water. Twitching the flies will pull the legs back, and when tension is released the legs will kick back. This looks like a struggling hopper or other insect. Sometimes, I'll fish them like a Diver by pulling them under and then letting them float back up. The small head and buoyant wing allow the fly to do this. The noise can pull fish to the fly, and this a good technique for moving or still waters. In rivers, when the current pulls them under, you can strip them in. They may be taken as a streamer, migrating nymph, or crawfish.

Madam X, Parachute Madam X

I've adapted Swisher's Madam X design to imitate many fish foods. I don't think there is a rubber leg color that I haven't used, and with all the good dyed hair, almost any insect can be simulated. I fish blue damsel, salmonfly, golden stone, cricket, hopper, caddis, and dragonfly versions of the Madam X, and I even have weighted ones that are used for crawfish and shrimp patterns. They have fooled plenty of trout and warm-water species. The fly is so adaptable.

Doug Swisher grew up in Bay City, Michigan, and learned to fly-fish when he was eight. He graduated from Michigan State University with a degree in

Swisher

(tied by Doug Swisher)

MADAM X

Hook – Mustad 94840 standard dry fly, sizes 6 – 18
Thread – Yellow 3/0 Monocord
Tail and body – High quality deer or elk
Rib – Tying thread
Wing – High quality deer or elk
Head and over wing – High quality deer or elk
Legs – Two strands of white rubber secured to make X shape

PARACHUTE MADAM X

Hook – Mustad 94840 standard dry fly, sizes 6 – 18
Thread – Yellow 3/0 Monocord
Tail – High quality deer or elk
Abdomen – Tying thread
Wing – High quality deer or elk
Parachute post – Phentex Yarn or polypropylene
Thorax – Peacock herl
Legs – Two strands of white rubber secured to make X shape
Hackle – Grizzly

mechanical engineering, and in his first career, he lived in Grand Rapids, Michigan, and worked for Westinghouse, Dow Chemical, and Spaulding Fiber. Even with a real job, he spent a great deal of time on the water.

Along with his fishing partner, a dentist named Carl Richards, they became enamored with the intricacies of the aquatic insects upon which trout feed and how to better imitate them. They spent considerable time researching, collecting, observing, and photographing the insects and in so doing became very knowledgeable. In 1971, the research went into their book, *Selective Trout*. This book quickly became the bible for anglers interested in becoming better hatch fisherman and also learning why certain patterns do or do not work. *Selective Trout* also started Carl's and Doug's writing careers, and between them they have written or co-written seventeen books and videos. These books cover the gamut of entomology, fishing strategy, casting, and saltwater fishing. Their book, *Fly Fishing Strategy*, written in 1975, is still one of the best general fly-fishing books on the market. In 2000, their revised edition of *Selective Trout* was published. This included important updates that had been picked up over the previous twenty-nine years and introduced another generation of anglers to this important work.

Doug has been fishing in Montana since 1959, and in 1979, Doug moved out to Hamilton to be closer to its premier trout streams. Since the 1960s, he has taught fly-fishing schools, and he now specializes in fly-fishing schools, a fly-fishing school for couples, and casting schools. Until recently, he also had a captain's license in Florida and, in conjunction with Captain Bob Marvin, started the first saltwater fly-fishing school.

Doug came up with the Madam X in August 1982 as an attractor fly for his home river, the Bitterroot. This fly made perfect sense on this water, with its good population of stoneflies, caddis, and terrestrials. From here, it quickly spread throughout the West. It was the first trout fly that I can think of that used the rubber X legs, and now this is a common trait on many of our flies. The big hair, foam, and rubber-leg flies that are bread and butter on western rivers have roots in the Madam X. This fly is versatile, and you can change the color, size, and dimensions of it to match any number of situations. Swisher himself has caught trout, salmon, steelhead, warmwater species, and even tarpon, sharks, and barracuda.

Not many flies have that resume. Elk and deer hair are the standard wing, but Doug also uses turkey, calf tail, partridge feathers, and synthetics for the wing. In June 1989, he added the Parachute Madam X, or PMX, to his arsenal of effective flies. A parachute hackle was added to the basic X concept to make the fly more buoyant and better for skittering. This fly has also become a mainstay in the West and around the world.

Doug keeps coming up with great new fly ideas. I like his Velcro-headed streamers and baitfish. Like many good tying ideas, it is so simple. His flies are commercially produced by Montana Fly Company, which also sells some of Doug's innovative materials, like his Rub A Dub dubbing. This has fine rubber mixed in with the rabbit fur. It makes a buggy-looking and effective nymph or leech.

For almost forty years, Doug Swisher's imitative and attractor flies have been landmark patterns and have led the way in fly design and effectiveness. ◆

AL TROTH

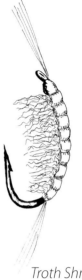

Troth Shrimp

IT IS HARD TO IMAGINE THE WORLD of fly fishing without Al Troth's flies. Many of them are worldwide standards. The Elk Hair Caddis is the first pattern people think of when an adult caddis is mentioned, and his style of Pheasant Tail Nymph is as common in a Pennsylvania fly box as a Montana one. Al and his flies have successfully bridged the gap between East Coast and Rockies fishing, and his fishing and flies have a basis in both regions. Although his Elk Hair Caddis was first fished in Pennsylvania, its wing was fashioned from a western elk. Al is one of the few tiers whose patterns became western standards long before he moved to Montana. Most of his famous flies were created to fish the waters of the Greater Yellowstone area, but have a worldwide appeal. His patterns and fly ideas are deeply entrenched in my fly boxes.

I can remember the first time I saw a fly tied by Al Troth. I was tying custom flies for avid Jackson angler, Bob Esperti, and I met Bob at his house to discuss a fly order. He brought out his collection of fly boxes and showed me some of the patterns he fished. In his collection were fishing flies tied by Jack Dennis and Al Troth. I picked up the slack as Jack and Al became more in demand and shorter on time. I had tied and fished some of Al's patterns for years, but it was amazing to see the original patterns tied by a legend.

The flies weren't complicated, but they were immaculate. It was obvious that a practical, serious fisherman had tied the flies with a high level of skill, and that he had a good grasp of the necessary features in a fish-fooling fly. Through Bob's fly orders, I was given the chance to improve my versions of Al's flies and learn more about some of Al's other patterns.

I interviewed Al in 2001 for a Japanese magazine article. I had chatted with him before at a Federation of Fly Fishers Conclave, but this time we talked for quite a while. He had plenty of knowledge and was willing to share it. My favorite Troth story is about his first full elk hide. Around 1955 or 1957, when he was fishing on the Madison, he was talking to a rancher, and the rancher asked what kind of hair he used on his flies. Al said he used elk on many of them. The rancher said he had an elk hide stuck on the barn and he could have it. It hadn't been tanned—it was just left to dry from last fall's hunting season. It was rock hard and stinky. Al took it anyway. Elk didn't live back home in Pennsylvania, and a quantity of flies could be tied with an entire hide. He took it to MacAtee Bridge on the Madison and dangled it in the water suspended by a rope. He would check on it every day. After eight or nine days it softened up and lost the worst of the odor. The elk hide made the trip back home to the East Coast. Inadvertently, this chance encounter led to his method of straightening elk hair. He would tack it up on his garage, spray it with a hose, then comb it straight when it was saturated and leave it to dry.

The universal popularity of Al's flies comes from their practical design. The flies that Al ties are beautiful but don't require excessive steps, complicated techniques, or hard-to-find materials, and they catch fish. The list of his innovations is very long. His plastic bag carapaced scud is the first nymph that I can remember with a plastic back. This feature has evolved to become commonplace on our modern patterns. The Elk Hair Hopper, a forty-year-old fly, was one of the first non-hackled, realistic hoppers. It was designed to sit low in the water like a natural. It was also one of the first to incorporate legs into the design. The Hair Spider was originally tied in the early 1960s as a skating fly for crane fly hatches in Yellowstone National Park. Good, long, stiff hackles are hard to find for skaters, so Al flared a clump of hair behind the eye of the hook and made a perfect hackle for this style of fly. His Yuk Bug is the ultimate chuck-and-duck-out-of-the-boat fly and is probably the ultimate big stonefly emerger. His Mac Salmonfly and Mac

Troth Shrimp

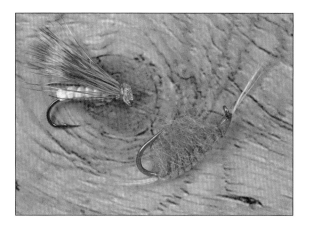

Troth Elk Hair Hopper, Troth Shrimp

Hoppers used polypropylene cord on the body for flotation, durability, and profile. Al was one of the first to incorporate visibility features into many of his dry flies. His Gulper Specials are tied with white, orange, or black post to enhance their visibility in different light conditions. He also uses bright overwings on his stonefly and hopper patterns. His Gulper Special led to my Two-Tone Parachute.

Troth

TROTH SHRIMP (tied by Al Troth)

Hook – Dai-Riki 135 scud #10 – #18

Thread – Olive 6/0

Tail – Olive hackle fibers

Antennae – Olive hackle fibers

Rib – Mono

Body – Seal mixed olive, red and orange. Spikey fibers on #10 and #12 and fine seal on #16 and #18

Back – Plastic bag strip

TROTH ELK HAIR HOPPER

Hook – 2XL streamer, sizes 8–14

Thread – Yellow 3/0

Body – Dyed yellow elk hair

Legs – Red biots

Wing – Dark elk

Head – Butts of wing

Al was a high school shop teacher in Pennsylvania, and he spent many of his summers fishing the waters of Montana. After years of recreating in the West, in 1973, he made the big commitment and moved to Dillon, Montana, with his wife, Martha, and son, Eric. He supplemented his guiding income with substitute teaching and fly tying. As the years progressed, he became in high demand for his skills and became recognized as the expert on his home waters, the Beaverhead and Bighole. In addition, his knowledge extends to many of Montana's best waters.

In 1996, at the age of sixty-six, Al retired from guiding. This wasn't due to a lack of enthusiasm, but he was diagnosed with Parkinson's Disease. He finished that year of guiding so as not to disappoint his clients, but Al still spends time on the water for himself. His son, Eric, now continues Al's tradition of guiding.

Al continues to tie despite his difficulties. The volume may not be there, but the quality still is. His flies are sold exclusively in shadow boxes, as befits a tier of his stature. To make tying easier, he has adapted his tying techniques and tools. He has made special tools, such as an armrest to make his arm steady, and he has purchased different tools to simplify his needs.

Another artistic side of Al that many anglers don't know of is his photography. His photos are amazing, especially his underwater shots. To get the gear he wanted, he built his own underwater camera housings for his Nikon camera. Al also has written articles for fly-fishing and fly-tying publications, and he has had his photos published in magazines. He is accomplished in all of his endeavors.

Wherever you fish East or West, Al's flies are welcome travel companions, and are sure to own some serious real estate in your fly box. ◆

INDEX